THE ART OF CONVERSATION

THE *MODERN LIVING* SERIES

THE ART OF CONVERSATION

BY

D. ERSKINE MUIR

ODHAMS PRESS LIMITED

LONG ACRE, LONDON

FIRST PUBLISHED 1953
BY ODHAMS PRESS LTD., LONG ACRE, LONDON
ALL RIGHTS RESERVED
PRINTED IN GREAT BRITAIN
IN LINOTYPE CALEDONIA
BY ODHAMS (WATFORD) LTD.
WATFORD, HERTS
T.453.PQ

395

CONTENTS

views — example: Brains Trust where old asked young their views — talking to the old — patience — love of old to recall past — do not worry or startle with new ideas — sympathy and affection — enjoyment of old and young in joint conversation — may be rare — depends chiefly on attitude of old — young must not be bored — amiable comparisons — let young decide what they wish to talk about — no impatience on either side — interest from variety of experience on both sides.

INTRODUCTORY

CONVERSATION can be "one of the greatest pleasures in life." It should be a pleasure within reach of us all, since everyone has a tongue with which to talk. Yet too many people uneasily feel it is a pleasure they miss. They find it difficult to begin, or to carry on, a conversation. How often one hears people say: "I'm dreading going to that party—or meeting So-and-so—because I never know what to say." Yet all human beings depend for their friendship and their knowledge of others on speech. We are not in this world in order to "delight in solitude." We wish to make friends, to get to know other people, and we wish to enjoy ourselves in the company of others. So most people would like to experience the enjoyment of conversation, to share in this "great pleasure," but they do not know how to carry on a conversation.

Yet conversation is not a gift, it is an art, and therefore can be learnt and practised. Those who have no natural gift for it can, with some trouble, learn to improve. This little book is an attempt to help such people, to show what may be called the rules (vague though they are in some cases) which help to make good conversation, and thereby it is hoped to make this wide range of enjoyment easier to obtain.

CHAPTER ONE

IT TAKES TWO TO TALK

*Need for exchange of ideas — no monologues — interest
in others' points of view — no capping of other people's
experiences — need to develop conversation from particular instances to subjects of general interest.*

CONVERSATION should be the exchange of ideas.
If we are to enjoy good conversation that is the
ideal at which we must aim. For one of the most
important points is to grasp the fact that conversation
is based on exchange. We wish either to learn something,
and so develop our own knowledge, or perhaps to learn
to understand something of the person to whom we are
talking. We shall learn nothing whatever unless we are
willing to listen to others, to allow them, indeed to induce
them, to explain their views or give their experiences.
It is quite useless if one person talks away, monopolizing
attention and preventing anyone else from joining in.
There is then no exchange, no development. However
well that individual may be talking, others should be
allowed to play their part, which indeed they probably
long to do, since no one really very much enjoys hearing
someone else "hold forth." Macaulay was considered a
brilliant man, and a brilliant talker, but he spoilt the
pleasure of others by never giving anyone else an opportunity; he was described as being "a roaring torrent, not
a meandering stream of talk . . . he astonished, and
instructed, but seldom amused and still seldom pleased
. . . and his 'flashes of silence' were too rare." The modern
counterpart of Macaulay may perhaps be familiar to us
as the person who will say: "Oh, I know all about that,

10

I can tell you exactly, etc., etc." "Ah! Now let me tell you what is my opinion. I've taken an interest in that for years, and I say, etc., etc.," and so goes on to pour out an unceasing stream, to which we may listen with interest, but sooner or later we will long to interrupt and have our say. Talk carried on along those lines is not conversation, and therefore, though we *may* enjoy hearing someone else, we would really enjoy ourselves far more if we were taking a full share. Here we can see the approach to what probably is the first important rule about conversation, namely, that in talking to others we have to consider them and not concentrate on ourselves. To be a good conversationalist one must be unselfish, ready to find out other people's views, and to be sympathetic in the best sense, that is to say, to enter into what other people think and to be prepared to listen and so come to understand them. This is fundamental. We all know that we do not enjoy simply listening to what others have to say, and yet one must listen in order to understand. All parties to conversation need to have this idea of joint enjoyment firmly fixed in their minds. It is the foundation on which all the rest is built.

There is a practical point to notice here. It is not a help to conversation if when someone tells of an experience you at once reply by relating one of your own. Very often the temptation to do so is irresistible. "A" will begin to describe something that has just happened to him or something he has heard. If one instantly replies: "That reminds me that when I went to . . . etc.," from then on you get no further. In the last war how tired one became of hearing of "the other person's bomb," it became dull to try to cap one experience with another. Yet again and again in general talk people go on describ-

ing their own adventures or telling what happened to
them, each person giving an account of himself. Now
one must listen politely—even if with secret impatience
—to the accounts of others, but inwardly one is not
deeply interested. For as we are all, in general, chiefly
interested in ourselves, we usually listen only until we
can tell our own story. Talk along these lines does not
take us very far, and in the end we only feel we have
not had a very interesting time. Therefore, it is best
really, when this recounting of experiences begins, to
make a great effort to try *not* to cap what has been told
by a story of one's own, but to deny oneself that pleasure
and try to take the conversation along wider lines.

To give a practical example: suppose one has gone to
a party (large or small) and someone begins to say how
he had seen an accident, or perhaps had a thrilling
escape from some danger—a danger which may range
from a motor-smash to meeting with a fierce dog—don't
then give as vivid and exciting account as you can
manage of how *you* had a similar or worse experience.
If you do that you will only tempt someone else to "go
one better," and instead of conversation you will only
have a series of descriptions of different events. Instead
make an effort, involving perhaps some mental struggle
with yourself, to give up your own interesting tale
(which, of course, you are longing to tell) and see if
instead you can get a discussion on perhaps either the
need for better traffic rules—or the rights and wrongs
of keeping fierce dogs as guards. Given any sort of help
from the others, you may really develop the conversation.
You may in the one case go on to transport, its various
kinds, its future possibilities, its help in understanding
other countries through travel, and so on. In the other

you may progress from "watch-dogs" to the evil of dogs in towns or to the preference some feel for dogs over humans; or by a different route from "watch-dogs" to dogs as guiders to the blind, and you may find yourself in the end going on from blindness to the way man can overcome all sorts of disabilities and how modern life seems then to have shown progress. And there you have accomplished your purpose, your conversation has gone on from one point to another, touching on things which are of general interest, and enabling different people to add their contributions. Everyone who has been able to join in has been pleased, and in the end one may perhaps have achieved the grand object, everyone has enjoyed himself, and parts in a glow of pleasure at having had an "interesting conversation."

To sum up, this is the first lesson in the art, to bear in mind the share others must play, to listen sympathetically, to avoid thinking and expressing too much of one's own ideas or experiences; in short, to be perhaps consciously unselfish, and so to arrive at exchanging ideas.

CHAPTER TWO

DIFFICULTIES IN CONVERSATION

Necessity for joining in a conversation — silence on anyone's part spoils conversation — difficulties due to shyness — or to ignorance — talking about ourselves — difference of tastes — need for sincerity and frankness.

THERE is another aspect to this basic idea of exchange. For some people find that their greatest difficulty is that they cannot easily join in a conversation, they cannot make, they think, any contribution to the talk.

Now, in general conversation (that is to say, conversation at a party) the old saying "speech is silver, silence is golden" is completely untrue, silence on the contrary "becomes a crime." Everyone ought to be prepared to play his part and take his share. Everyone at a party will look with disfavour on the "dull" guest who sits dumb and makes no contribution. Every host or hostess will feel despair as he or she looks at the silent guest, feel bitterly how heavy is the weight which now falls on others, will secretly but burningly feel the wrongdoer ought to be making some sort of effort. Worse still, such a silent guest will be inevitably considered as a person who will not be asked again; and if such a reputation grows, then few and far will be the invitations the poor dumb wretch will receive.

Dr. Johnson expressed his views on this matter with his usual forthright bluntness when, speaking of a young lady with whom he had been in company, he said: "She, sir, says nothing. A talking blackamoor were better than a white creature who adds nothing to life and, sitting down before one, is desperately silent." It is indeed a wearisome effort to try to talk to someone who will not respond. Here again is another aspect of the need for unselfishness.

People may be silent because they are shy and feel unable to call attention to themselves. Shyness is perhaps the most usual cause of people not venturing into conversation. Yet it is actually a difficulty which is comparatively easy to overcome. Efforts can be made, and here there is the consolation that practice really does enable one to get over this disability. Just as public speakers learn to overcome nervousness, so the individual can learn to overcome shyness, by forcing themselves to talk. They will be encouraged to find how the effort does become less, and they can spur themselves on if they realize that unless they make that effort they are putting an intolerable strain on others. They must try to take the view it is simply not fair to sit silent and give no help. Some people never overcome their inner feeling of nervousness and shyness, but they *can* learn to conceal it and to make this effort to talk which is a social duty. And once the first painful effort has been made, and the first few sentences have been uttered, so the shyness will melt.

In the same way, anyone who is trying to talk to a shy person must persevere, be gentle, try to set the other person at ease, and in this case perhaps be prepared to do rather the larger share of the talking. If those awful pauses come, when the shy person seems unable to respond, then the bolder talker must make a fresh effort, probably try another topic, but always hoping to encourage the other. It is a test of kindness and of perception, for one must find a subject which will not alarm the nervous by being too difficult, and must also try to find out what can be discussed. It is no use, for example, to ask a nervous girl: "What do you think of the country's finances?" or some such portentous subject. Ask her instead if she likes the decoration of the room, or the pictures on the walls, she can answer that, and if then encouraged she will be capable of going on to talk of the way she would decorate a room herself, and the pictures she likes. Or a shy young man will be made miserable if his hostess asks him for his ideas on anything —he dare not give them—but he may blossom out if he is asked mildly how he is getting on in his work, or has he been doing anything of late in the way of concerts or films. From that he can be persuaded to talk of the kind of music or film he prefers.

That happy individual who has a natural gift for conversation is always a welcome guest, for any host or hostess rejoices in someone who can be relied on to "make things go." Such a person may sometimes be implored to come to a party "because the others are rather sticky and we want you to come and brighten things up." Well, unselfishness may be called for here, too! It may be an effort to go to a party which is expected to be dull, so as to oblige a friend! But those who are good at conversation, and who can talk easily on most subjects, will recognize that such a gift carries with it some obligations. And if they really use that gift with sympathy they will generally find they are rewarded, and the "dull" party will prove a success. One needs to stress the word "sympathy," for anyone who tries to talk only for effect, to dazzle by showing his brightness, will fail. The others in the party will be perhaps alarmed, perhaps made more reluctant to talk themselves. Success in enlivening the conversation will come only if the good talker manages merely to stimulate the others and bring them out.

Some people who are not naturally shy and who can talk away quite happily when they feel the conversation is on a very easy level, sometimes will not talk if they think the subject is "beyond them." They think they cannot produce anything very interesting to say, they feel themselves too ignorant, or perhaps "inferior" to the other talkers. They think that they cannot "live up to the level" of the conversation.

For example, someone who does not read very much, or who reads only light literature, or detective tales, may find himself with people who begin to talk about more serious books. Then the "light" reader may feel out of his depth and sink into a rather unhappy silence. Or someone who has never travelled finds the conversation turning to places other people have seen. But he must pull himself together, try to be brave, summon up his ideas, and see whether he can possibly say something on the matter under discussion. He must try not to mind if what he says seems rather "feeble" or even stupid. He can often disarm criticism by saying apologetically: "Well, I'm not very good at that, but what you say is very interesting," or: "Well, I'm afraid I can't rise to those heights, but I like hearing all this," or: "I'm very ignorant on all this, but I enjoy being told about it."

Actually almost everyone can venture an opinion, or explain his point of view. Everyone can try to contribute toward keeping a conversation going by expressing what he thinks. If the other talkers seem too "clever," they will in reality be interested to hear the ideas of an "average" person. Even the most brilliant talkers are often interested and are helped by finding out what the "ordinary" person thinks. They may even need to see that their talk is not clear enough, that they must make their views better understood. Human vanity being what it is, a very clever person probably enjoys every now and then making his ideas clear to someone less gifted. (If he has a nice disposition, he will feel a little of the glow of wellbeing in enlightening someone more ignorant!) The best kind of brilliant talker, too, will never wish to appear "superior." He will not be scornful or snub the other, he will try to take up the point and get at the other's difficulty. He will try to extract from the less good talker whatever he can of interest, and encourage the other. In other words, here again is unselfishness, on the one hand for the brilliant always to consider the less good talker. And for the shy or more ignorant there should perhaps be willingness to face making a rather poor (or as he may think stupid) remark, making a fool of himself in fact in order to show some sort of response. For if people do not respond at all, conversation can go no further.

Perhaps here we can pick up a hint. People sometimes say: "Well, I'm too stupid to understand that," or, more aggressively, "Oh, you are too clever for me!" That acts as a full-stop. It is just as easy to say: "I can't quite understand that," or "That sounds difficult to me, can't you make it clearer?" These phrases will help the other person to keep the conversation going and the two respectively will come to understand each other better; and to understand something about the other person is one of the chief aims and certainly the source of some of the greatest pleasures in conversation.

Human beings gain immensely from learning to understand others, and they can best do this by talking together. Most people realize the pleasure and satisfaction they feel after having talked to someone and seen into that other person's heart and mind. To feel in sympathy, to discover tastes in common, gives a sense of delight. Yet one misses this if one is intent only on expressing one's own ideas. Here again is the emphasis on exchange. We need to explain to each other just what we feel and why we either share the same feelings, or differ.

Lord Chesterfield gave his son the advice: "Never speak of yourself at all," but we may doubt the wisdom of this advice. If we are trying to make contact with someone we must, in getting to know him, talk about ourselves, always of course bearing in mind that we are aiming at understanding each other, not just expatiating on our own personalities. Chesterfield here gave another piece of advice. If you do talk about yourself, "do not," he said, "fish for compliments." Often people unconsciously do this, by talking of how they have behaved, or of how they pride themselves on their good characteristics. ("Well, I know I take a broad-minded view," or "I'm not like some people, I wasn't going to haggle.") This is not, of course, a serious fault, but again human nature makes the listener almost unconsciously observe the faint note of self-praise, and that is not an endearing trait. Leave such things unsaid, and if you really have behaved well your listeners will see it for themselves and think the better of you. In brief, do not comment on your own behaviour.

Again, in conversation you do not get very far if, in reply to something said, you simply remark you feel just the opposite. To take a very ordinary example. You, who live in a town, may be talking to someone who lives in the country. You do not want just to say: "You live in the country? Oh! I couldn't bear that, I like a town." That really means first that you do not care about the other person's choice of a place to live, and secondly you have made him feel rather snubbed by your remark, since it implies what is good enough for him is not good enough for you. Instead, if you ask why the other one likes the country, and say it is interesting how people are divided on the question of town and country life, you will find out something about the other person's tastes and interests. You may find, for example, that he deeply loves beauty in nature, hills, fields, trees and flowers. You may realize you yourself find beauty in a town, in a street where light is reflected from wet pavements, or in the silhouette of buildings against the sky, and you may end by realizing you both love beauty and appreciate what you see that is lovely around you, only you find it in different ways.

Possibly both the city and the country dweller, on the other hand, find they share one thing in common, say a love for bird life, and the town dweller here can "keep his end up," for birds can often be studied in an interesting way in a back garden, as well as on a moorland, and the mutual love of bird life will prove a shared interest.

Quite often, if you seem to have a totally different outlook on life, when you try to get at the reasons for another person's views, you may discover after all that you can have more agreement than you thought. You need patience, but your patience is rewarded by the sympathy you can express in each other's outlook on life. Indeed, this is an instance of how, by approaching conversation from quite different sides, you can become interested in another person; you can each find what you have in common.

We shall go into this more fully later, when we deal with the subjects on which people often talk.

This brings us to another point. In conversation we should be sincere and frank. If you say what you honestly think you make conversation real and true. Everyone respects an honest opinion, but if you try to say what you think will just please others, or if you have not the courage to express your own opinion, if you think you cannot stand out against what everyone else is saying, and you simply fall in with the views expressed though in your heart you disagree, then you bring something unreal into the talk, and what you say will have no real value. Often when you are at a party, or even if you are just two people talking together, you may not like to stand up for your own view, and you may (rather feebly, perhaps) seem to agree. That will not take the talk any further. If you have seen a play, or read a book, or seen a film which is being discussed, and you really disagree with the view being expressed, but do not like to say so, it is a mistake to pretend to fall in with the other view. It is far better to be brave and speak out what you really feel. For one thing, no one minds honest dissent. For another, in a general conversation, where all opinion seems to be going one way, if you are courageous and speak up you may often find that others also privately were not in agreement, but were too timid to speak, and they will then pluck up courage and join in and you will get a real discussion. As one man put it: "I do like people to be frank and say what they really think, even if I disagree with them; that's interesting, but if they just pretend to agree that's boring."

Here we get, perhaps, a conflict in our minds with our humility. We may really feel we do not know enough, that our opinion is not worth having, that the other people know so much more. Well, if you are trying to have a conversation, your "ignorant" point of view, if you really believe in your opinions, will have worth and the others will enjoy talking it out with you. Do not let "false pride" keep you silent or prevent you speaking. Take the risk, chance being thought rather "stupid." In short, do your duty and try to talk!

CHAPTER THREE

FAULTS TO BE AVOIDED

*Faults in conversation — aggressiveness — boring other
people — dangers of telling anecdotes — dangers of
relating one's own experiences — of trying to be "smart."*

HERE we come to another aspect. Nothing is more
fatal to conversation than aggressiveness. People
are "put off" or frightened by sharp or violent,
almost bullying statements. It annoys or alarms if a
speaker breaks out: "I think that's utter rubbish!" The
reaction to that remark is either resentment or a feeling
of being crushed. It does not endear anyone if he says:
"No sensible person thinks that," or: "I don't think you
know much about it or you wouldn't talk so," and then
proceeds to "lay down the law," which means he expresses
his views and treats you as a fool if you try to argue
and ridicules whatever efforts you make to explain your
own ideas. Reasonableness is a prime necessity. Anyone
who is dogmatic, who just states a case and cannot see
there is any doubt, or anything to be said on the other
side, spoils all talk, for in talk there must be give and
take, and we make no progress by mere assertions.

Again, the over self-confident and assertive person runs
the risk of becoming a bore, and a bore kills all conversation. People simply do not enjoy hearing someone
talking away and assuming everything he says is right
and interesting. It is dull just to listen to someone who
can only see things from his own point of view.
Whether it is a stream of talk on the lines: "Well, what
I always say is that those fellows have no sense at all;
why, it's dead clear, etc., etc.," or if it is an account of

exactly what the speaker felt and said while watching a football match, or what he thought about a radio programme ("I thought it all utter rot from start to finish; why, that fellow can't, etc., etc."), the conversation becomes a monologue with the bored listener drearily trying to put in a word every now and then—"Oh! yes," or "Really?" and lapsing into either a gloomy or a politely hidden boredom.

It is politeness that matters here, and the need to notice how people are taking the stream of commentary. Good talkers will pull themselves up and pause to see if the other is enjoying himself. Some people, after an outburst, will realize this and say: "But I'm talking too much, what do *you* think about it?" and then the situation is saved. They may even go so far as to say: "But I'm afraid I'm being a bit of a bore." The best answer to that is to say: "Well, you know, I can't agree with all you've been saying," and then try to get your oar in, and the person who is really wishful to "have a conversation" will then grasp that it takes *two* to make a good talk and will allow you to take your share.

Sometimes, too, you may notice how someone, describing an event he has seen, really describes chiefly what his own feelings were. "Well, when I saw that child falling under the car I felt absolutely faint. I just shut my eyes, I couldn't open them, I felt I just couldn't bear to look, I can't tell you how awful I felt," and so on, when what we really want to know is what happened to the child. Make it a rule, if you are describing something exciting which you have seen, to stick to describing it and do not go on endlessly about your feelings when you saw it. Again, one constantly finds oneself ready to reply to the relation of some experience by giving a parallel one of one's own. It is almost irresistible if you are given a vivid account of someone's experiences on a journey, or in a queue, or even in dealing with some domestic catastrophe, to reply: "Why, yes, when I was, etc., etc.," or "My brother had just the same experience when he . . ." There is a sort of fascination in this exchange, and of course it may be useful in setting up a feeling of shared experiences. But the danger is it may go too far, and one cannot go on for ever with one similar case after another. Once you have made contact, warmed to each other by recounting your own story, then make an effort and get away from it.

Conversation may also be thought of as a kind of game, aiming at enjoyment by the players. In this sense it must be "light," that is to say, gay and cheerful, with as much fun as can be introduced. It is, of course, no use to set out with the intention of having an amusing conversation. Any amusement must come as it may, incidentally and arising out of what is said. In fact, it is fatal to set off with a fixed intention to "tell comic stories," or to try to be amusing by "smart" remarks. Funny stories are a pitfall, since in the first place they may not amuse others. A very good one, clearly marked out to amuse everyone, is rare, and can naturally be used—provided it is not dragged in at all costs. In the second place it is not always so easy to repeat a good story well and effectively, and one which can in the telling fall flat is disastrous. "Smart" remarks, too, may be a snare. Of course, it helps to make talk bright and sparkling if someone throws in a provocative or even an outrageous remark. A rather gloomy conversation on capital punishment was given a sharp twist when the question was put: "Do you approve of hanging, as the means of carrying out the death sentence?" and the answer was: "I think it's far better than the guillotine; I should prefer to be left all in one piece," and another then chimed in with the need, in medieval executions, for skill on the part of the executioner, the conversation winding up with a choice of people one would select as one's executioners. Of course, here the rule has to be observed: "suit your conversation to your company." If the conversation is really between people who know each other well, and will not misunderstand wilful remarks, or the putting forward of wild theories, then the fun can be fast and furious; but if you are with people you do not know very well, an effort to be very "smart" may be misunderstood and you may either be taken to mean seriously what you intended to be a joke, or you may be put down as heartlessly frivolous or cynical. Be quite sure that the company does not misunderstand the tone in which you speak. Be sure you do not hurt the feelings of those who were taking the matter to heart. Sometimes those genuine efforts to amuse or to lighten a topic which has become rather heavy may lead one on to say "bright" things which afterwards one regrets. One may realize one went too far, spoke too lightly. You can pull up and say: "But I don't mean that really," or: "I oughtn't to say that, I've let myself be carried away"; you can only judge of that if you are alert and ready to notice quickly exactly how others react to your efforts.

Again, a sharp, clever comment on any individual is often the cause of later repentance. We are liable to say something rather amusing but perhaps rather unkind and our words leave a sting. The words may hardly have left our lips before we secretly wish we had not spoken in that way. It is, however, a great temptation to produce an effect and to raise a smile by a pointed remark. Here we just must try not to speak too hastily, and the simplest way to avoid such mistakes is not to rush in and say what later we will regret. Equally, it is disastrous in conversation about personalities not to say what one thinks so as to be always "charitable" ("I never like to criticize other people"), for if we only say what is agreeable or kind we falsify all comment. Perpetual praise of others can hardly be always sincere. Adverse comment, if made, must be genuine, and all we need then care about is that it is not expressed spitefully or violently. No one really would say, if someone's name comes up: "Oh! I simply hate him, I think he's the most frightful person," or: "Well, after the way she behaved to X or Y one can't trust her an inch." Everyone hearing that would feel you were so prejudiced it would be no good talking further. It is quite fatal to discuss either public figures, or individuals one knows, if the criticism gives the idea of prejudice or malice. It just puts a "damper" on the conversation, and anyone who once gets a reputation for malicious or unkind conversation, however amusing and clever, will end by being avoided, and will never find people willing to talk openly and freely to them. "They say such spiteful things, and they give things such a twist, I don't like talking to them. You know they'll probably be saying the same sort of thing about you to other people," or: "It's no good trying to talk about any public leader—they're so hopelessly prejudiced and believe anything against him." In other words, there is no pleasure to be obtained from conversation with this disagreeable flavour.

CHAPTER FOUR

HOW TO HELP CONVERSATION

Need to develop conversation — follow up leads and bypaths — grave and gay conversation — depressing talk — telling a "good story" — talk about persons — about subjects — difficulty in starting a conversation — possible openings.

A FUNDAMENTAL thing in good conversation is that when two or three persons are talking together they should let one subject or point lead to another. The talk should be like a ribbon gradually unrolling, or like a stream flowing along. It should twist and turn, always moving on, not staying stuck in one place or always repeating and returning. ("Well, that's what we said before," but if we've said it once we shouldn't be back-repeating it.) Conversation should move on, developing on new lines as one thing leads on to another, and the talk branches out, often most unexpectedly.

You may start from a quite commonplace beginning to find in the end you have reached something very different. One actual experience was this. Three or four people began to discuss a film they had seen. In the film the "hero" committed suicide. That led to a discussion on suicide, was it ever justified, and so on to people doing what they thought wrong for the sake of someone else— and the question as to whether that was right. In fact, it ended up in a talk on right and wrong, good and evil. That would not have happened if the talkers had just stuck to the film story, but they went on to talk about the problem raised in that film and then to the problem of real life—than which few things can be more interesting. You may notice, too, that those are matters which can be talked over by everyone, however varied may be their abilities, or their education—for they are subjects everyone can understand and can discuss at his own level. They can be talked about just as much in a simple as in an advanced way.

In general, conversations which leave a sense of thorough enjoyment, that feeling which makes one think: "I did enjoy that talk or that party," are cheerful, gay conversations. Some people are lucky enough to have a light touch and to be naturally amusing and able to give a sparkle to any conversation. Of such people we think: "They really are fun, they make a party go, they make one feel brighter." Someone once said of a friend: "To talk to him is as good as a day at the seaside."

That is something we can aim at, or perhaps it is better to say we can try not to be depressing, not to leave our friends tired or a little flat after a talk. A great many people simply do not realize that to talk always of things that have "gone wrong," always to take a gloomy view, always to talk of things which are irritating, or to complain of the world in general, and one's own unfortunate experiences in particular, does have a flattening and depressing effect on others, and no one enjoys that. People prefer to be cheered up, and to have a conversation that leaves them enlivened and stimulated. If you find yourself in company, or just talking to one other person, and the talk seems to be getting on depressing lines, you can check yourself and try to turn to something more agreeable. Or you can say more or less firmly, to your companion: "But let's leave all that and find something more cheerful to talk about." Or if you've been lamenting over the state of the world, you can try to discuss how the young generation do not seem to be depressed, they have youth's greatest gift, hope—and perhaps you can get on to the qualities and advantages which youth possesses and which we can admire and from which we can gain ourselves hope and encouragement.

Here we may return, in more detail, to a point mentioned before. People who want to amuse and entertain others very often think the best way to do so is to tell amusing stories or anecdotes. It will always be arguable whether this really does help on the conversation. It may, of course, if things are going rather stickily, if conversation seems to have come to a dead end and there is one of those frightful pauses and silence. But so much will turn on the story. Far too often a "good story" has gone the rounds and people have already heard it. For instance, how often someone will begin: "I read a good thing in the paper today," and quite forget that other people have in all probability also read that story and do not want to hear it repeated. It is possible, of course, to get over this hurdle in another way. You can ask: "Did you see that thing in the papers today about . . . ?" If the other has not, you can go ahead. If he replies: "Yes, I did," you can discuss why it was so amusing and to the point, and so on. Sometimes, too, a "good story" does achieve exactly what was intended. It does lighten the talk and often breaks the ice and, by making people laugh and relax, gets things going. Strictly speaking, stories ought to fit in with what is being talked about. Thus if you are talking politics (and perhaps people are getting rather heated), if you have heard an amusing political anecdote, or seen an amusing cartoon, you can ask if the others know it, and *if they have not* you can tell it.

However, to tell a good story just as if it were out of the blue does not lead to conversation. A man may begin: "I heard a good story today," and insist on repeating it. (He may add: "Stop me if you've heard it," but he does not wait for you to do so, nor have you usually the nerve to say you have.) Generally, if we ourselves like telling stories we only listen and wait till we can tell our tale. If the company in general—like men forgathering in a pub—really enjoy "swapping tales," well and good. They will be thoroughly happy and amused, but they have not been carrying on conversation. Their tales take them no further. If you are at a party, or talking with someone who will insist on relating endless anecdotes, you may determine that this is not the kind of talk you want. Then you must use courage and also tact. You must try to check the flow, or steer the conversation away. You *may* be able to do this by seizing on something in the tale. To take a very rough example: if the anecdote is one of those eternal ones about a Scotsman, well you can make a feverish dash at it and get on to the Scots in general, their characteristics and their country. But, in general, the habit of telling good stories is a stumbling block in the way of good conversation.

Again, to go back to talk about persons. If you wish to acquire the art of good conversation you need to grasp the idea that the best conversation will arise when people are not talking about persons they know, or who are public figures (whether politicians or film stars), but when they are discussing subjects. Yet sometimes it is impossible to keep on talking about general things and it is a relief to move on to talk about people. On public figures we can talk readily, we have our own ideas, and, as these personalities are known to all, everyone will have their opinions and can back them up. But if we find ourselves talking about individuals we know we may find ourselves caught up in difficulty. Talk about one's friends and acquaintances may be just mere gossip, or it may be criticism, or more often, as the majority of people are kind-hearted, simply praise ("I do think she's sweet," or: "He's a grand fellow"). Obviously that is not conversation. It may, again, like the "story," serve to fill a gap, or to bridge over an awkward place, but it clearly cannot lead very far. We have to accustom ourselves to the idea that good talk must in the end be about subjects —in a party, subjects, moreover, of general interest.

Now naturally, clever and highly educated people score in conversation, they have little to fear here. For they have many interests, much knowledge. Yet even in this respect the "clever" person may not always do so well. It is not enough to be highly intelligent or learned, it is equally essential to be adaptable, to be able to talk readily on all sorts of subjects. High praise was meant when it was said of one individual: "He is splendid at a party, he can talk about anything, from economics to horseracing." That power of finding different subjects to talk about over a very wide range is clearly easiest to those who themselves have wide interests. Yet actually those lucky individuals are only doing what we can all do, even if on a small scale. They are talking about things they find interesting, they are fortunate because they have widespread interests, and fortunate because, being themselves highly intelligent, they can do it very well. But even those less gifted have their interests;

everybody has. We have a choice here, and a choice everyone must make when they set out to talk. We can either talk about the things which interest us, and see if the other person responds, or we can start off by deliberately trying to find out first what interests others. In either case you must sooner or later adapt yourself and aim at a "give and take" attitude. You can "have your go" at the thing you are keen about, but you must remember the other person wants equally to get on to his favourite topic. You must go to and fro, each getting his turn.

Everyone has some special subject on which he is keen. It may be sport, or gardening, or going to the theatre. It may be the study of history, or collecting books about the place in which he lives. It may be modern art or architecture, or the keeping of budgerigars. Once get people on to the things which really interest them, and they will talk with enthusiasm.

The difficulty here is, of course, to make a beginning, to track down the subjects each likes to talk about. To be completely practical, if you are with someone you have not met before, you must just plunge in, like an explorer, and try one path after another. You may have to begin quite bluntly with asking a question: "Are you keen on . . . this, that or the other?" This is to ignore Dr. Johnson's remark: "Questioning is not a proper mode of conversation." Johnson meant personal questions about an individual's family, etc., which today we call being inquisitive, and in that sense possibly we agree with him. Yet even then we have to modify his words, for sometimes the only way to make contact with a stranger is to find out if he has a family, where his home is and so on. But if we are trying to find out what are our new acquaintance's tastes we shall do better. Once we have been told what our companion is keen about we can easily go on to discover why that is so. What makes him take up that hobby? And from his reply we can probably find something about his life, or his history, or the place where he is living, that helps us at once to understand him and be interested in his way of life.

CHAPTER FIVE

FINDING A SUBJECT

How to find a subject — think of one beforehand? — starting a conversation with a formidable person — finding a mutual interest — beginning with books — or hobbies — can one talk about religion — or politics — or "shop"?

PEOPLE who have been invited to a party, or to meet some particular person, and who are nervous and aware of the difficulty they find in talking, do quite often try to think out beforehand something about which they can talk. For example, one lady who was shy, and felt herself a poor talker, worked hard on the daily newspaper "looking," she said, "for something interesting she could bring up." She happened to be unlucky, for another guest, also shy, had had the same idea, and, getting to work first, brought up each topic our poor friend had hoped to introduce. The idea of "thinking something up beforehand" may possibly help those who believe they have too few ideas and will feel dreadfully at a loss. More probably they will waste their time. It may turn out quite hopeless to introduce the subjects they "got up," and in any case a subject so prepared will be likely to show it has been prepared, it will be laboured, it will not represent the person's ideas. Far better to take a risk, to hope there will be an easy opening, and above all not try to reproduce what one has memorized.

Again, some people are in themselves alarming, or you may quite unnecessarily dread talking to them for fear they are "too clever." This reputation may arouse miserable fears in those who have to try to talk to them. You may hear someone beg: "Oh, don't put me down next to So-and-so, I'm frightened of him. He's too clever!"— or: "He's so difficult to talk to, I never can think of anything to say." Well, the only thing here is to face misfortune boldly. It *is* bad luck to have to cope with a formidable person. You can only do your best. Try not to be driven, by sheer nervousness, into talking rubbish. Try to think: "Well after all he's a human being" (and you may perhaps rather maliciously comfort yourself by thinking, most people like talking about themselves), and if he will not make a start you must just go ahead. Perhaps you will do best if you stick to a simple opening. You probably feel too nervous to be capable of starting off on anything "original." So you can fall back on the familiar opening: "Have you been doing anything interesting since I last saw you?" or "Don't you think this"—and insert here any public event or discovery —"is interesting?" You may be crushed with the reply that it does not seem very interesting to your partner, but the chances are that if he disagrees it will launch him off on to why he disagrees or disapproves. Then, again, you may pick up a crumb of comfort, for people often get intense enjoyment in explaining why they disagree with whatever is being said or done.

Such "openings" apply to people you already know, and if you are dealing with milder individuals you probably know in advance that they have some hobby or pursuit which they will enjoy talking about. Generally, having once made a start, you will both "warm up" and go along happily. Remember, however, if you can, that here, as always, you want to prolong the conversation, to get it moving from one point to another, going perhaps from the particular to the general.

Thus, to take a homely example, many people take an interest in gardening, and you will know in advance if your friend devotes himself either to roses or to vegetables. You have your cue ready for you. You begin: "How are your peas coming along?" but having shown kindly interest in those peas, you want to push ahead and talk, say, about whether it is worth while growing peas at all. Is it any economy, or even if no cheaper as regards peas for the kitchen, is it worth while because a garden is an interest? Then can come the flower or vegetable discussion—and perhaps visiting a local show —and perhaps trying out new things seen in another part of the country, or read about—and so an endless topic blossoms out. Or, as another little instance, for those who specially love growing flowers, you can get on to flowers to grow in the winter, and from then to books on winter gardening, and you may find you enjoyed discovering Mr. Beverley Nichols in one of his novels giving some useful practical hints on winter flowers, and from there you may get to books on gardening, or delightful accounts of gardens in books. Having begun with, say, winter jasmine, you may, if you are lucky, find you both love the description in Jane Austen's *Mansfield Park* of how Aunt Norris succeeded in "cadging" "a very beautiful little plant which that nice old gardener would make me take."

Another very usual subject which often serves as a beginning is books. We shall deal with this more fully later. Taking it as a possible opening, however, a great many people can make a happy start simply by asking: "Have you read any good books lately?" This is always easy, since any reader is always on the look out for something fresh. But here is a pitfall, too. If you want

to talk to your companions about a book which you have
enjoyed, but which they have not read, do not be
tempted to induce them to read it by giving a description
of the plot and the characters. For either they "don't like
that sort of book," and whatever your enthusiasm may
be they really do not intend to read it, and will be
unmoved by your account, and bored to death by your
description, or they do intend to read it when they get
the opportunity, and you will then spoil their pleasure
by telling them beforehand what happens. No! In
beginning to talk about books the best thing is to
discover as quickly as you can some book you have both
read, and say you liked it (or disliked it) and what do
they think about it? Then you are off. Readers, indeed,
score heavily in the game of conversation. Someone once
said to a friend: "I wish I'd read as many books as you
have. You always seem to find plenty to talk about."
But then, great readers are the lucky ones, for they have
the path made easy to begin a talk, and they will have
plenty of ideas with which to follow up their flying start.

Yet those who are not fond of books have no cause for
despair. Tastes do differ, and if you even establish at
once that your new acquaintance "doesn't care for
reading" you can drop that subject and fish for another
clue. Hobbies? Sport? Gardening? You can say cheerfully: "Well, if you don't care for books, what are you
really keen about?" And if you are so terribly unlucky as
to be faced with a feeble conversationalist who may only
answer: "Well, I don't know quite," you must simply
persevere, peg away until you find something, for something there will be, which can bring a gleam of interest
to your partner's face.

Here is another minor point. You can always tell from

the expression if what you are saying does rouse and interest others. It may seem a small thing, too easily overlooked. Yet, if you stop to think for a moment, how easily ought one to detect the faint boredom coming over people's faces, and even more obvious the lighting up, the sparkle which has given to successful conversation the name of animated.

We now come to more dangerous ground. Often it is said that neither religion nor politics is a subject for general conversation. Lord Chesterfield laid down the rule: "Religion should never be discussed in mixed company." The reason being that it is both a subject on which people feel very deeply and on which they vary strongly. The danger which is dreaded is lest people's most sacred feelings will be outraged in conversation. Of course, this is perfectly true, and it is therefore equally true that religion cannot be discussed except by people who know each other well. (And usually such a subject can only be discussed between a very small group of three or four persons.) Yet Lord Chesterfield's rule need not be accepted as unbreakable. People who really enjoy talk on serious subjects, and who are also interested in religion, can and do talk about it. They may talk, on rather general lines, of the position of the Church today, of their feelings about Church services, and so on. Or they may discuss the problem of morality, of "predestination," of divorce, and many such difficult subjects, and those who have fundamentally different ideas may get stimulus and help from discussing together something which is of vital interest to them. This does presuppose conversation among real friends, not acquaintances. Equally, such conversation is possible only if the persons talking together respect each other's convictions and are capable of discussion without hurting feelings. They must use restraint, keeping calm and being able to criticize and to meet criticism without wounding. More people than might be supposed are interested in religious and moral problems and would like to talk about them. This is perhaps specially true of young people who want to face their difficulties and, if they can, resolve them, and they can and do find help in discussion.

Politics are now much more widely accepted, and here the same points apply, only matters are somewhat easier. In these days most people, of all ages, have political ideas. It ought to be helpful to discuss such ideas with those who hold different views. For in that way one's own ideas may become clearer and one can learn to understand and respect opposite views. The reason why people say "we mustn't talk politics" is simply because so many cannot "talk politics" without losing their tempers. If we can only keep self-control and remember not to be aggressive, or bluntly contradict, we can make "politics" a very interesting and stimulating topic. Perhaps one simple thing is to bear in mind the old saying "opinions differ," and cling to the fact that everyone has a right to his own opinions. What is wanted is to talk, with calm, as to *why* those opinions are held. If people "never talk politics" they never hear the other side.

One can learn so much by hearing and answering. One ought to be *ashamed* to say: "I can't discuss politics, I just lose my temper." Intolerance is, as always, in conversation the real crime. It may be difficult to be reasonable and see the other case, but it ought *not* to be difficult to be polite, and if one is polite one exercises self-control, and neither is offence given nor does the conversation degenerate into mere abuse of some view or some set of people.

Another point can be made here. Actual experience often helps to understand political views. For example, anyone who has been down a mine, or has been in contact with mining conditions, or has been to a mining village, can bring practical knowledge which may modify views held by people who only "go by what is in the newspapers." And people who think the universities are strongholds of snobbery and the home of the reactionary well-to-do would possibly change their views if they were talking to someone who knew at first-hand how different matters are, with so high a proportion of state-aided scholars. Here is one of the other things which make political talk rather difficult: people so often are not talking about what they know, they are too often swayed by ideas picked up at random. Ignorance leads here to bitterness. The only way to avoid that is to bear in mind that there always is "another side," and in discussion to see if that can be given consideration. For everyone is aware that where there is a quarrel, or a difference of opinion, there must be something to be said for one's opponents. On these lines people can talk and be interested in political subjects with perfect safety.

Talking "shop" is often reckoned to spoil conversation. For it may be unutterably dull for the rest of the company to have to sit by and listen to two "experts" discussing their subject. Yet this dictum needs to be modified. It may be really interesting to hear people who are masters of their subject talking together. It may be possible, too, for the listening company to "chip-in" and ask for something to be made clear to *them,* or they may even have the courage to object to the views being expounded, being always prepared to be thoroughly "put in their place." Good humour naturally helps here, and the daring interrupter can try to pacify the expert by saying: "Don't despise me as an ignoramus; but do let me put in a word for the ordinary person." If in a mixed company two experts, delighted to meet each other, cannot resist plunging into a highly technical talk—say on some scientific subject, or legal or naval point or the technical side of mountaineering—then the others must realize they cannot even listen intelligently, and they must simply leave the other two alone and themselves get on with their talk of the things that interest them. If the two experts in their turn realize the rest of the party are there to enjoy themselves and deserve consideration, they will, after a satisfying bout on their speciality, remember their obligation as guests and set to work again to join the others in more general talk. Indeed, never to go on too long with one topic is clearly a rule to be applied universally.

If one finds oneself set down to talk to anyone who wants to talk their "shop," being oneself quite ignorant on the subject, then a sort of "receptive-unselfishness" may bring its own reward. For, being ignorant, it may be a pleasure to learn, but one must be prepared to do so, to listen with sympathy because the "expert" is so keen, and to try oneself to take an interest. It *may* be dull to listen to a man who is utterly absorbed in explaining how he sails a boat, or how he binds books, or how he has found some rare plant, but it is possible both to learn a little of something quite unknown to oneself, and possible perhaps to be interested in the personality which shows itself in the course of the talk. To be ready to be interested is an art that can be learnt.

CHAPTER SIX

TALKING ABOUT BOOKS

*Talking about books — different types of books —
popular books that arouse feeling — need not to check
talk by "superiority" in taste — talking about novels —
plots and characters — translations — dialect novels —
talking about classics — about specialized books —
travel, natural history, etc. — pleasures of similar tastes
— amusement from opposite views — friendship
through books — talking about plays — modern —
classical — types of plays.*

As an art, conversation will gain if it is based on
subjects which it is really worth while discussing.
Clearly the best conversation is found where the
most able people are talking about worthwhile things,
such as literature or art or philosophy. But we cannot all
reach such heights and, in addition, conversation, even
in the most brilliant circles, cannot be kept all the time
on such a high level. So we come to the consideration
of subjects on which ordinary conversation can be based.

One of the easiest and most fruitful subjects is books.
Anthony Hope once made one of his characters say: "I
wish you would read a little sometimes, your ignorance
cramps my conversation." Quite clearly, if you read,
though only a little, you have the key to a whole world,
the world of books.

Some people read a great deal, and they are fortunate,
for their talk can branch out in many directions. They
can discuss novels, or travel books, or essays and so on.
Even for them there are pitfalls, and here the rules which
ought to guide conversation by the brilliant may prove
most useful to those who read less.

In talking about books no one need be ashamed of his taste. Probably the vast majority of readers do not read "serious" books, probably not even the English classic novelists. But as subjects for conversation we have one distinction between levels. The highest level will talk about the best in literature, but the other levels can talk with enjoyment about the books that please them. Only, to be interesting it must be real talk, not a few remarks (such as: "I thought it lovely," or: "I didn't think it very good," or "don't waste my time on that sort of thing").

Talk on modern novels is often the most usual topic, and as such novels generally have not very much value as "permanent literature" anything said of them cannot usually be very absorbing. The vast flood of novels pours out every day and every week, you read them and forget them. But while you will not get the best talk about such books, still there they are, a ready and easy subject for light conversation. So let us think of talking about a book which is very popular and is being widely read. It is no good taking too high a line over such a book. A "best-seller" has pleased a very great number of people, therefore clearly it has something in it which appeals to the average person, who forms the vast majority. Naturally then such a book which "everyone is reading" can be talked about by the ordinary reader. Usually it is a novel, and we can observe it is also usually a novel with a great deal of incident. People who unconsciously find their own lives rather humdrum get enormous exhilaration from reading something which takes them right away from their own lives. They enjoy, too, the touch of romance.

If there is such a book to discuss, all sorts and kinds of people can share the pleasure they obtained when they

talk about it to others. Even those who do not care for
or appreciate such literature can still find in it a basis
for discussion. For example, such novels as *Gone With
The Wind*, or *Forever Amber*, or *Jamaica Inn*, can be
talked about eagerly and with relish by those whose
taste they suited. But in a "mixed" company, where some
perhaps consider such novels not up to their own level
of taste, it can be interesting for those special individuals
—casting aside any tinge of "superiority"—to talk
amiably with those who enjoyed it, perhaps on the lines
of finding out just why these books had such an appeal.
It is no good to say proudly: "Oh! I think that's not my
type of book," a comment which stifles all further talk
by its implication that the book is not worth discussing.
It is so much pleasanter to "suit your conversation to
your company" and say: "Well, I don't exactly like that
kind of book, but tell me what you enjoyed in it." Nor
should the timid let themselves be overawed. They can
take the firm line that they do not care for "difficult"
books, they prefer "light" reading. Or they may be able
to explain why they enjoy something which takes them
away from ordinary life, and into a world which seems
more colourful and more exciting. Again, as ever, courage
is called for, based on truth, for one must come out into
the open and be ready to say what one appreciated, even
if one has an uneasy feeling of exposing oneself. After all,
it is possible to say humbly: "Well, I'm afraid I haven't
very grand taste in books," or, if one is taking a different
view from the popular one: "Well, I am rather a heretic
in these things, I can't enjoy them." It is necessary, too,
to stick to one's ideas, and not be like the lady who said:
"Oh! Don't you think it was good? Well, I shall have
to take back what I said."

Or, to take a different type, one can readily get a conversation going by discussing a book which rouses feeling. Political books such as *Inside Europe* or *I Sought Freedom* are widely read because they stir up deeply felt convictions on political subjects of general appeal. Naturally such books are better, on the whole, to talk about, as they both produce more lively discussion and also lead on to talk about subjects allied with the book in question.

In either case the great objective is to create a real discussion, not to crush those who differ, but to talk over the reasons why we liked or disliked, why we agreed or disagreed, why we were interested or bored. Dr. Johnson said: "That is the happiest conversation where there is no competition, no vanity, but a calm quiet interchange of sentiment." It always depresses people terribly to have a book they have enjoyed condemned out of hand as "poor—worthless—just rubbish." Their vanity is hurt, because their taste is made to seem so poor and the critic has let vanity in his judgment run away with him, and he has forgotten to be polite and considerate toward other people's tastes.

Talk on these lines really develops into talking about tastes, and incidentally reveals a great deal of the character of the people who are talking. If we are going to discuss a novel, we can find a great deal to say if we go about it in the right way. We can discuss the plot. Was it well constructed? Was it convincing? Did it matter if it was improbable? Is a good plot essential, or is the development of character more fascinating? This may involve us in discussion of different types of novel, especially today, when some have no "plot" properly speaking, but may describe the events of one day, or the life stories of a number of people meeting by chance in, for instance, a jury-box or on a bus. Those readers who do not usually read that type of novel but stick to the plain "story" may, through such conversation, be tempted to try this other type, and discussion like this may rouse their curiosity and give them something fresh to try.

Of course, too, one can, and usually does, discuss the characters in books. If one wants to make the talk interesting it may be a help not to be content with saying: "I thought A was such a nice character, I simply loved him," but to talk about whether, put in his position, one would have behaved as he did. Sometimes a heroine maddens one by the mistakes she makes—and the same applies to a hero. Well, would we have done the same? One curious point which sometimes emerges if a man and a woman are discussing a novel is that they may have very conflicting feelings towards the heroine or hero. The author, as can be told from the whole tone of his book, intends you to like his heroine, to feel sympathetic toward her, and yet women will say: "I couldn't really like her. I felt 'against' her all through the book." Possible examples may be (though many will not agree) Irene in the *Forsyte Saga*, whom many women do not really like; or, in more recent fiction, the heroine in Joyce Cary's *American Visitor*, whom practically all women dislike but whom men admire. To get on to those lines in a discussion can be very amusing and very provocative. Men may say it is mere jealousy on the part of the women, but that it not true, since women love and admire a charming heroine such as Elizabeth Bennett or Anna Karenina.

Novels are the most widely read of all books, but there

are large numbers of people who enjoy as well other types, such as travel books, books of Arctic exploration, books about mountains, "country" books and so on. If you can discover that your companion shares one or other of these tastes you can be completely happy together. And, in addition, so often in mixed company, others hearing your talk will be drawn in and perhaps say: "That sounds interesting, I think I should like to read that." Do not be afraid then to talk of a book rather off the ordinary track. Branch out and give variety.

Another subject which lends itself to discussion is the question of translation. People who can read a book written in a foreign language often object that one essential of a good book is its style, and this obviously is lost in a translation, however good. Others maintain that as the majority cannot read foreign languages, a translation is justified because it does enable everyone to enjoy the masterpieces of other countries. The same applies to the "rendering" of old masterpieces into modern language. As this subject is controversial it is a good subject for conversation, provided that those who do know foreign languages show great moderation and tact in not emphasizing their advantages.

As another suggestion, we can talk about novels written in dialect—Scottish, North Country and what the B.B.C. has called "Somerset." For here, too, there are violent differences of opinion which can give rise to heated arguments.

The greatest pleasure probably comes to those who can enjoy what may truly be called a "literary conversation," meaning by that conversation about good literature. Many, for example, have a profound love of the English classic novelists, Dickens, Thackeray, the Brontës, Jane

Austen, etc. One can be endlessly happy when one meets a kindred soul with tastes that match one's own. You can discuss which novels you prefer, and in detail the scenes which stand out. Take Thackeray, for example, for he in particular has scenes which stamp themselves on one's mind. Or one may criticize his "moralizing," or appreciate his style. Then there is often a quarrel between those who cannot read Thackeray but who "love" Dickens, and irreconcilable views can be thrashed out. People disagree, for instance, so profoundly over Jane Austen. Her true lovers can argue endlessly as to which they consider her best work, and they can quite passionately discuss the character of Fanny in *Mansfield Park* and the change that might have been produced had she married Henry Crawford. Or, as another example, a very bold enthusiast over Jane Austen's works once startled other equally ardent admirers by putting forward a heretical view of *Pride and Prejudice*, namely, that most people were carried away by Elizabeth's charm and wit and did not see she was "not good enough" for Darcy, being pert, sometimes rude and often too pleased with herself. This may be accepted as a possibly extreme instance of how, in discussing such well-known books, a conversation may be made more amusing and more stimulating if a bold unorthodox view is put forward.

Discussion of very specialized tastes may and often does produce a very quick glow of enthusiasm. For instance, people who at first sight seem very unlikely to share such a taste discover they enjoy such books as *The Hunting Wasp*, which probably enables them to find out they share odd tastes in the world of natural history, they like toads, or snakes or bats—and there they feel an immense bond. Or, in a very different direction, they may enjoy Victorian literature, such period pieces as the works of Mrs. Oliphant or Charlotte M. Young or Marryat or Ballantyne. Rare though these cases may be, there is nothing so warming to the heart as to find a fellow enthusiast. An American (a most unlikely person one would have thought) found himself suddenly completely at home in an English circle because he, having been brought up by an old aunt, had read and loved this brand of English Victorian book. Such surprises may meet us in any conversation and produce the warmest and most delightfully friendly talks.

Indeed, this is the secret of the pleasure found in talking about books. One discovers similarity of tastes. In this way conversation fulfils its deeper aim, it enables us to catch a glimpse of someone else's personality and character. For the kind of books one reads and loves is a guide to one's character. You can not only "tell a man's character by the company he keeps," but also by the books he reads. From the delightful experience of finding one has similar tastes in books, one can go on to lay the foundations of a real friendship based on the knowledge that such discussions inevitably give the clue to character.

Perhaps all this may seem rather vague, for it is not easy to pin down the way to talk about books. But one can suggest that such conversation should tend toward talking, in the case of a particular book, about that book as a whole, taking in different points about it. One can talk, too, about the different kinds of books, and so can discover special tastes, and the main features of such talks should be the discovery of tastes, whether opposing tastes or ones that are shared.

All that has been said about books applies equally to conversation about plays. Naturally, people meeting together will tend, if the conversation turns on plays, to begin to talk of new plays they have seen. One may begin by discussing the most striking scenes, or the particular actors or actresses. Then there remains, beyond those easily dealt with aspects, the play itself. Was it well constructed? Did it fall off toward the end? What was the author trying to do? Did he succeed? Again, one discovers the kind of play preferred. Do we like plays to be realistic (a picture of daily life) or romantic, taking us away from ordinary humdrum life to a dream world where things happen which are improbable but pleasing and exciting? Many people have very strong views on this. Some dislike intensely plays which reproduce the lives we all live, and give an exact picture of the contemporary scene with which we are perfectly familiar. Others enjoy the play which turns on character, the development of character, or more usually the effect of one strong character on the lives of others. Or the play which turns on such a subject as a parent's possessive love (and this can range from Strindberg's *Father* to *The Silver Cord* or *Washington Square*). These different types of play always give rise to a good deal of discussion and start people expressing their ideas.

Again, do we enjoy a modern historical play (and the success of Shaw's *St. Joan* shows how many can)? As always, the best plays tend to produce the best conversation. We do not get very far by discussing a farce. There is not much to discuss, but we can have glorious conversations on classics, such as *Othello* or T. S. Eliot's plays, or a very "up-to-date" "problem" play. Here, above all, it is absolutely necessary to be sincere. One should never be afraid to take a view not generally shared. Boldly admit that one found a play which has been much praised dull, or too difficult. Do not pretend, for if you do your sin will find you out. The persons to whom you are talking will realize that you are not whole-hearted, your comments do not ring true, and your pretended agreement will soon show its weakness. Then the conversation will tail off and cease, for no one wants to discuss anything if there is not honesty in the discussion. Say what you think and try to give, as clearly as you can, your reasons for thinking so. This is a universal rule, and holds good for talk about every kind of play. For we may not all appreciate difficult and highbrow plays, and we can talk just as happily about plays of a slighter character provided we really do talk about them sincerely. Even the "popular farce" can be interesting if we do not just say: "Oh, wasn't that scene funny? It made me laugh till my sides ached," but if we can, however light-heartedly, explain why it is a relief and an amusement to see people rushing in and out of the wrong bedroom doors, and why cheerful nonsense can be such a source of pleasure. The eternal rule comes into force: always say what you truthfully feel, and always try to expand a bald, bare statement as to what you like or dislike into an explanation as to why you feel that way.

Of course, too, it seems a truism to say that the best plays provoke the best talk. There is more to discuss in *Hamlet* than in *Call It a Day!* But people may avoid talking of the performance of a Shakespeare play because they feel everything has been said already. That should not be an obstacle. The very bold and provocative may, in order to make a conversation "go," put forward a variant of George III's honest remark: "Shakespeare? Sad stuff! Sad stuff! Only one mustn't say so." Without going as far as that (though again one can argue that throughout the eighteenth century Shakespeare's plays were considered "sad stuff") one can still argue and bring forward the just criticism that many of Shakespeare's plays are of an inferior calibre, and can argue that there is not much to be gained by having them performed. That will clearly provoke discussion. And again, with so many different presentations of Shakespeare, people who see different productions can argue away happily on their respective merits.

As to actors! Quite unending will be the talk as to the preferences people entertain: there is no need to do more than mention any actor or actress's performance and ease and animation break over the conversation.

CHAPTER SEVEN

TALKING ABOUT FILMS

Easier subjects for those who do not care much for books or plays — conversation about films — topical — comparison of types of films — how not to talk — recounting plot — no one wishes to hear of films not seen — discussion on effects of films — limitations — books as films — Shakespeare filmed — photography — scenery — radio — difficulties over words.

PERHAPS some people will feel: "This is all too difficult for me, I don't read that kind of book, or go to that kind of play." Well, that may be so, but all the same these ideas will help us even if we do not rise to such heights. For those who do not read many books may instead be people who read magazines or light papers and so on. Here there are often subjects for conversation—articles on people's daily life, arguments in the "Letters to the Editor," photographs of something which catches one's attention. Indeed, because these periodicals have a wide popular appeal and deal with topical matters they may be a great help, partly because so many people read them, but partly because they tend to pick out subjects which will interest the majority. So, for those who want to find a subject for conversation it may be a good idea to look at such publications and try to decide what there is in them to discuss. If, as often happens, there are accounts and pictures of the daily life of workers in special industries, say, for example, a miner or docker, then one can discuss such work and perhaps compare it with one's own occupation, talk about the advantages and disadvantages and so on. And often

"Letters to the Editor" in any paper (illustrated ones or local newspapers) may prove a mine of subjects, since one generally either agrees heartily or disagrees violently with the writers. For instance, the person who wants all dogs forbidden in towns because they foul the streets, or the writers of frequent outbursts on those children who do not give up their seats to older people in buses and trains, or (rather more fascinating) the letters on the paper-picking habits of tits, or the appearance of rare birds in Britain. It is wonderful how many subjects one can find in this way.

Similarly, most people go to the "pictures" and therefore here is a common interest ready to hand. There are always the first-rate films which are widely seen and enjoyed. Here again one must always bear in mind that though naturally one will tend to say: "Didn't you think So-and-so was wonderful?" that is not enough. You need to go on and develop your ideas. Was the film actor or actress really interesting? Would one have behaved as he did in the circumstances? Does one sympathize with him and see his point of view? Does one agree with the choice of such actors to play those parts, and so on. Or, going on from that, does one like films which reproduce real life as we know it, or prefer something which we cannot know and experience, such as films about the jungle or the Arctic or stories of disasters at sea? And, eternally, why do so many people enjoy films of violence or crime? Is it really "bad for us" to be thrilled and excited by such subjects, or is it simply the need for something more exciting than we generally find in our own lives? Or we can talk about so-called "historical" films, such as those based on Nelson and Lady Hamilton, or "biblical" ones, which may lead to all sorts of arguments. Is it a good idea to take subjects such as "Samson and Delilah" or "David and Bathsheba" and so perhaps lead some people to read the original story, or do we think it a wrong idea to "cheapen" such subjects? Most people would find they had quite a lot to say here. Again, obviously the film never keeps strictly to the original true story, and we can discuss whether this is important or not, and whether it is justifiable to twist events which really happened, so as to give a more dramatic effect, even if it does falsify the real story. Are such films, even if they are not accurate, a help to our imagination? We could never in any case see with our own eyes those distant countries, or perhaps be able to re-create for ourselves events long past. We can argue, therefore, whether it is better to get an incorrect idea, as is more often the case in "historical" films, rather than have no idea at all of the events and the people dealt with.

As a special example, for those who have seen Shakespeare on the films, there is always the chance to dispute whether Shakespeare *can* be filmed. Does his poetry suffer from the "film setting," the music and so on? Or, even if it is so different (and, of course, so much is always left out, or the film would be too long), is it worth while producing a film which seems to "take liberties" with a great poet, just in order to bring his work before people? There are many people who would never dream of reading Shakespeare, or going to see one of his plays in a theatre, but who will be attracted to a film because of the popular actors and actresses who star in them. But lovers of Shakespeare may be indignant over the changes made by the films and will talk hotly about this.

The one rule which should always be observed is,

never to attempt to describe the events of a film to someone who has not seen it. How often does one hear people
begin: "Oh, it was lovely! It was about a man who
was . . ., etc., etc., . . . and then the girl says . . ." and
then follows every detail of the plot and every event.
Well, that will almost certainly spoil the pleasure of
anyone who means to go and see that particular film;
they do not want to hear it all beforehand; they want to
be surprised by what does happen in it. Moreover, it is
terribly dull to listen to anyone describing in words a
film which after all is meant to be *seen*.

Then, more seriously, one can talk of the effects of
films on the audiences. People will always argue as to
the effect of films of violence on children. Are those
effects bad? Do they really teach children criminal ways,
or do they simply give the clever, badly-behaved child
a ready excuse when he gets into trouble—"he saw it on
the films"? Or do children really come to no great harm
in this way, as they perhaps need the excitement which
in other days they got from violent "blood and thunder"
stories or detective tales? Do children as a rule identify
themselves with the heroic character and side against the
villain and so on? Does this prove these films do them
good, as the children take the side of right?

Less usually discussed, but a good subject for conversation, is the effect of the standard of life shown so
often on the films. That is to say, the "luxury," the
wonderful clothes worn by the women stars, the lavish
furnishings, the large rooms, the incredibly expensive
flower decorations and so on, all in the homes of people
who in real life we know could not have such surroundings. One can discuss whether all this elaboration and
costly surroundings are really effective. Is it convincing,

or, because we know that nowhere except in the film world are there such things, does it spoil the effect, as when a heroine in a wild jungle story appears always with immaculate "hair-do's" and wonderfully well-pressed clothes. Would we prefer to have "realism" with dirty, untidy explorers and their womenfolk? Or, alternatively, do we want to see clothes, houses, furniture, such as none of us experience in daily life? Do we, in short, need something different from our own lives and so want to see things we know do not represent what is real at all? Or is it bad for us to get an utterly false idea of how people look and live? We can be clear here that this is something anyone can talk about in the simplest way, such as the man who can begin: "Well, I think such pictures are a disgrace, just make girls discontented and want to look like film stars," and who may in this way provoke to discussion any of his feminine audience who enjoy seeing what they do not aspire to, or who may boldly assert they are helped in ideas of how to make themselves or their homes more beautiful, even if they cannot be as lavish as the film.

One can talk, too, about the interest of seeing films about other countries, and perhaps develop this, as so much turns on the way the film deals with it. For instance, sometimes a "short" which shows us Italian peasants cultivating their fields, and gives a picture of their village homes, or a film with mountain scenery, may not only be compared with our ways, but we may go on to discussions of the countries we would like to visit, and more generally to the need to broaden our knowledge of other people's lives.

If we see a film based on a book we can perhaps find out if the people we are talking to have read the book.

We can argue as to whether it is right for a film to alter the book, whether the "unhappy ending" of the original should be altered to please the supposed wish of the cinemagoer always to have a "happy ending," whether that is really so, or do people sometimes appreciate a "sad ending"? This may help us to go further, for we can discuss the enjoyment people find in something sad or tragic. People will often admit: "I like going to the cinema and having a good cry." Partly, it seems, people do not mind "crying" in a darkened cinema, and indeed at any sad part sniffs break out, handkerchiefs are produced, but the audience does not get up and leave, and these films are usually most popular.

It may be that in talking on this point we can induce rather shy or "sticky" persons to thaw when they confess they were touched by some episode. From there we can go on to try to find out why our companions were so moved, why is it so touching to see a man accept suffering or even death (as for example in the stokers caught below in a sinking ship or Captain Oates going out to die in the snow, or the policeman killed in doing his duty)? If we can go deep enough, or be brave enough to say what we think out loud, we can say that it does one good to see what ordinary human beings can endure quite naturally. Or, from the quite opposite point of view, we can say it is not good for us and we do not want to see represented the crimes or the vileness and cruelty of which mankind at its worst is capable. We can argue, less often perhaps, that when we see wickedness it makes us think and wonder why such things are done, and can they be prevented, and so we can discuss whether a horrifying film is justified for the reason that it rouses our social conscience.

If we do not like "arguing" about films, because that is a matter of different tastes, and though it does often lead to interesting discussions, yet some people cannot express themselves easily, or just do not like arguing, then we can more peacefully talk about the "photography" of a film, the beauty of the effects. If we have been lucky and have seen a film with good photography we can talk about the strange effects, such as the scenes in the sewers in *The Third Man*, or the staircase shots which are so striking in many modern films. Or, if we are not interested in that side, there is always the scenery in "outdoor" films, the animals in any jungle country, the mountains, or the many films dealing with the East and the desert. The mechanically minded can talk of films with aeroplanes. Indeed, if one takes the trouble, there are endless subjects to be found in the "pictures," but we must never be content either to try to *describe* what we have seen or to give only our point of view and not bother about anyone else's. Say firmly: "I enjoyed that part, did you?" or: "What did you like best?" Always, always, see that the talk does not get pulled up short by a bare statement: "I thought it pretty poor," or: "Oh, she was marvellous"—but go on, taking that just as a beginning, and try to discover what reasons the other person has for his opinion, or what his tastes are, and get a comparison with one's own likes and dislikes. In short, go on from one point to do with the picture to others.

Radio, again, provides all sorts of things to talk about. Naturally, perhaps, the best field for subjects of conversation is to be found in those programmes which are in themselves conversation, such as "Any Questions," or "The Critics," or, of course, the political or religious discussions. The famous "Have a Go!", too, will often be a good subject, for the lives and experiences of the people taking part can be talked about, they do so often give us an idea of such completely different lives. So many people listen to one or other of these items, and one can so easily say: "Did you listen to that this week? Did you think that bit was interesting, and did you agree with So-and-so?" Indeed, if we are going out to meet other people and feel nervous in advance and feel "hard-up" for anything to talk about it may be a good idea to make a special effort and listen to one or other of these programmes, whichever we prefer, and make mental notes: "That was a good point. That's interesting," and try to remember it as "something" to talk about. On more general lines one can start a conversation by asking if other people like "Variety" or the "Saturday Night Theatre" or "Studio Audiences," and if so, why, and if not, why not.

Here, therefore, is an easy way to start a conversation. "Did you listen to the wireless last week? Did you hear . . . ?" The shyest and most tongue-tied can both make a start in this way, and carry on from there. But, as before, never be ashamed of your taste. If you like variety or commentaries on boxing matches do not be ashamed to say so. On the other hand, do not be *any* sort of "snob," do not say: "Oh, that's too highbrow for me!" or, even more contemptuously: "Oh, are you one of those people who like highbrow music?" It is just as much of a damper to conversation, because it really means you think badly of the other person's taste—it is a form of rudeness, and a way of snubbing, though you do not mean to be either. Try not only to be interested in other people's tastes, but respect them. If you do, probably both of you, in talking it over, may resolve you will give the other person's programme a trial; and, in any case, if you do talk it over and say what you think, you will have found subject for conversation.

So, with films and radio as subjects which appeal to everyone, it is possible to find easy topics to start on and, with a little pains, ones which can enable everyone to develop along really interesting lines. One rather small point may be noticed here. Some people find they cannot talk readily because they have a poor vocabulary. Everything is "smashing" or "marvellous" or "horrid." They do not perhaps know a very great many words, or they may feel at a disadvantage because they do not understand some of the words other people use (and do not like to show their ignorance by asking). The simplest remedy (awful as it may sound) is to look down the columns of a dictionary every now and then and learn some fresh words. Two quite well-educated people once heard a lecturer complain bitterly how small is the number of words used in conversation, though English is an extremely rich and varied language. They bought a dictionary and used to read it aloud and so learnt the use of more words. That may be rather a strange way, and, of course, no one should use artificial language, but there is something in it. Luckily the blessed crossword puzzle has given many people a better vocabulary. If we do manage to learn to use more words our actual talk will be more interesting to other people.

CHAPTER EIGHT

HOBBIES

*Hobbies — infinite variety — gardening — flowers —
gardens and decorative arrangements — endless bypaths
here — sport — men's specialities — women's share and
enjoyment — many developments here — advantages
and disadvantages — other nations' ideas — discussions
on blood sports — on professionalism in sport — other
games — examples such as chess or cards — children
and sport and games — travelling — do not give a
long account of your travels — specialized tastes —
pictures — music.*

Now let us come to subjects which should help very many people, and in an easy way—hobbies. For here we find endless variety and also a fairly easy way to open a conversation. If we are with friends or people we know a little we probably know what their hobbies are. If we meet strangers we can ask them outright: "What's your hobby?" and not very many people will blankly say: "I haven't any." If anyone does, well you can say cheerfully: "Why, aren't you interested in anything? Well, I spend my time in . . ." and go on to try to interest them in whatever you do, and perhaps you'll end by inviting them to come along and see your roses, or your budgerigar that talks, or your collection of whatever it may be.

Still, you will be unlucky if you strike someone who has no hobbies at all, though perhaps people do not at first grasp how wide a field "hobbies" can cover, from stamp collecting to upholstering, from breeding canaries to drama, from collecting china to collecting match-boxes! Gardening comes to the mind at once as a hobby which is widespread, common to people with very different incomes and wages, and which has endless openings. So many people have a garden, and, however small it may be, once you discover they are keen on it you will have no difficulty. For you ask at first if they like growing flowers or vegetables, or fruit, and then you discuss how to get the best results, which plants do best and so on. Or you can talk about the colour arrangements of borders; is it a good idea to have, as few people do, a border or even a garden all in shades of one colour, blue or red, etc.? Those who live in towns and may have no garden can still have plenty to talk about, for many grow pot plants or ferns; and, indeed, new books are coming out now to deal with this "house gardening." Incidentally, it is a help here if we have read such books, or read the "garden notes" which most papers give now and which do include "pot plants and how to grow them." Besides this plain easy topic, one can go on to the question of cut flowers in a room. Should one have none at all, or a great many small vases, or stick to one or two large masses? Should one try to learn from books and magazines how to arrange them? Or will that mean everyone's flower vases will just follow a pattern, not one's own taste? These subjects naturally appeal largely to women; but, after all, men do love flowers, too, and the great shows prove how they can excel in arrangement. Indeed, here we could perhaps have a good conversation, with a woman trying to get a man to say just what he thought about this. Men used to be ashamed at the mere idea they should "arrange flowers"; but if they grow them, why not share in "arranging" them?

Practically all men, of course, can talk—and do endlessly—about sport. But we are trying to think of conversation which must mean "give and take." So, though two men can be happy over football and cricket, or boating or darts, if they are with women and girls they must make a little effort to bring them in, too. This is not as hard as it used to be; for besides going to see matches played, women do now listen to sporting events on the wireless. But just to go over the things which have happened will not be interesting unless everyone has watched or listened. Of course, women may claim that they have been trained so long to be "unselfish" listeners, to "let the men get on with it," but in the long run that leads to dullness. Men may start a conversation by talking of sport, to break the ice, but they ought not to go on just giving their views and ideas, they must be more unselfish themselves and more enterprising and ask the others what they enjoy and be more ready to let them "have a go." One must not, perhaps, expect too much, but since we do recognize the immense interest in sport we might possibly go on to talk about just that. Is it a good thing for a whole nation to be so taken up with sport? What about other countries? What do such nations as the Swedes, or the Danes, or the French care about? (One is told the French are as passionately keen on bicycle-racing as we are on football.) Do international contests or the Olympic Games draw nations together? Is professionalism a help to sport? Here are plenty of "sidelines" which can be the subject of real conversations that can be enjoyed by all those whose chief hobby is "sport."

Then there is, especially for country people, that very debatable subject of "blood" sports. Fox-hunting, stag-hunting, otter-hunting. Though here, if people have different views, and if they really know the subject, they will have to keep very firm hold of their tempers. The golden rule here, for those who utterly disagree, is to try to think: "Well, he's a sensible man, let's hear why he thinks that" and be prepared—on both sides—to listen without anger.

This subject of outdoor sport perhaps makes one think of the many hobbies open to those who love "natural history." Either birds in their wild state, or birds studied, as they can be, in towns. One can find out the books written nowadays on owls, or the cuckoo, or the blackbird, and so on. Those who vaguely like the "common" birds may, if they find themselves talking to someone who is really keen, discover there are these books, and be encouraged to read them and so develop that "hobby." There are town dwellers whose hobby is goldfish, or the breeding of tropical fish, and these people, once you find out that is their speciality, can make you enthusiastic and perhaps induce you, too, to take this up.

It is not difficult to find out all these things from anyone to whom you begin to talk. You just ask straight out: "Are you by any chance keen on—say—tropical fish, because I've just taken it up," or: "I'm going to a whist-drive this week, are you a card player?" Then you may find your new acquaintance is keen, too, and off you go to reach perhaps discussion of problems set in the papers and so on. If you draw a blank, and your friend takes no interest, then you must abandon that topic; do not bore him with an account of how you enjoy it and what you have been doing in that line. Try to find out—since he does not share that enthusiasm of yours—what he *is* enthusiastic about. You must try then to encourage him over *his* pet subject, and you will probably find it interesting just because it is something you have never studied. But, in any case, you need to bear in mind you must not "run a subject to death." You must not just stick to the one topic, you must move on and try to find other "hobbies." Otherwise you will exhaust your subject, and by talking too long about it end by becoming dull.

Another common interest is often to be found in what is grandly called "interior decorating," but which may also mean the pleasure of painting and papering and carpentering in one's own home. Men and women share this, and you can talk about whether, with married couples, it is best for the wife to choose the colour scheme and the husband do the "donkey work" of painting and papering. But, as always, try to have in your mind the rule: "Don't just describe what you have done." Do try to get on to something wider; for example, the need for different colours in rooms looking north from those looking south, the difference made to the look of the size of a room if one has plain walls or patterned, the help to be derived from books or from exhibitions, or possibly the bad side of this, since people just copy what they see or read, and so too many rooms are just alike—a table in the window with plant, "folk weave" curtains and so on. We may decide we like all this, and that taste cannot be individual since we must buy what the shops provide, but still we can talk about it. We can talk about "modern" furniture and decorations as compared with "old-fashioned." Probably everyone will have some pieces of furniture or china or pictures which they keep because of the associations, or which have real beauty, and one can discuss whether these can be "mixed" in with modern things. Plenty of ideas to be found here!

Travelling is another good subject. The lucky people may be those who can travel abroad. They will have endless notes to compare with others, the beauty of snow-mountains, or of lakes, or of great and famous cities. Those who take their journeys in Britain have plenty, too. Scenery, such as Wales or Scotland, or the peaceful beauties of the English countryside, or the wild moorlands of Yorkshire or Devon. Clearly, types of scenery, or what one prefers, can be discussed easily; so can "sight-seeing," which many, though not all, enjoy—castles, cathedrals, birthplaces of great men, and, nowadays, tours round historic homes. Clearly, most people enjoy giving an account of what they themselves have visited, and probably many conversations on this topic are just that—each in turn describing what they have seen. As long as "fair shares" are allowed all may go well, and perhaps listening to someone else one may get ideas for one's own next holiday.

One or two dangers should be noticed here. Never go on too long describing your *own* experiences. It is, of course, glorious fun for you to roam along happily going over every day of your trip round Cornwall, or every detail of what you saw when you went to France—but is it such fun for your listeners? Never let your talk be simply a case of comparing hotels or rooms or meals or prices; and, as a rule, if you are in your own home and have been talking about your last holiday, do not produce any photographs you have taken, unless, that is, your guests really ask to see them! A few may be interesting, but as a rule the majority, though *you* love to look at them because they recall so much pleasure enjoyed, will not interest others, who have not shared your experiences. Politeness may make them look at your photos, but a short spell and few photos should be the rule. Of course, to make your travels interesting to talk about you must have tried to see interesting things. If you just go for a motor-coach tour, and when you come to an ancient historic town only use your stopping-time there to dash off to the shops, you will have nothing to talk about. This is a case of perhaps learning to go "sight-seeing," because then you will have a store of things to talk about. If your mind and memory are full of interesting things you have seen, then you have a "hoard" to draw on when you want to talk to other travellers. You can always talk, too, about the people you have met and the different types you meet in different parts.

It is not necessary really to mention here such other subjects as pictures or music. Lovers of art who, when they go to any town, consider the local picture gallery to be the first place to make for, will always find each other out, and once such a strong bond as a love of art is discovered talk flows. You may need to take pains to find out such a taste, but usually it is pretty clear. People so often look round at the pictures on a wall, or they will volunteer that they have just been to see some gallery or exhibition. As always, do not be afraid of saying what suits your taste, only be sure you are not arrogant over this. It is no good being proud (as some are) of their lack of knowledge and bursting out: "Oh, I can't bear his work, it just doesn't appeal to me." Humility and a genuine wish to discuss are the best basis for conversation on art. The same, of course, applies to music.

CHAPTER NINE

MEN AND WOMEN

Men and women in mixed company — do they enjoy talking together? — attitude of each — timidity of women — cocksureness and condescension of men — playing up to men — talking down to women — subjects both find interesting — subjects each find boring — men tending to talk of their prowess or work — women tending to talk of their families — contribution of women in lightening conversation — or in providing unselfish listeners — improvements to be hoped for — sympathy — reason — have men and women different points of view? — conversational gains from this.

MEN can usually talk quite happily together, and women can talk happily with other women. There are plenty of subjects in which each sex is specially interested; for example, sport for men and clothes for women. Someone has remarked how fortunate women are in this respect, for practically all women in every part of the world take an interest in clothes and can talk about them anywhere and at any time. Men cannot be counted so lucky, for sport varies so much in different countries.

But when you come to "mixed company" it is not such plain sailing. Indeed, some people assert that men and women do not get the greatest enjoyment out of talking together! Probably that is not true, for there is an interest and a pleasure to be found in talking to "one of the opposite sex." "Mixed company" is stimulating, it is "fun" because of the different points of view held by man and by woman simply because they, as human beings, are different.

Men on the whole usually seem to have more confidence, to be more sure of their facts, to be better able to argue. This may sometimes mean they consider themselves qualified to explain everything, and to expound their views as the only sensible ones. Carried to its worst development, they may be too "cocksure," they may lay down the law and show that they consider themselves always to be in the right, and anyone who opposes them is ignorant and silly. Women, on the other hand, may be more shy, less willing to express their opinion, less able to "stand up to" a confident man. This, where it exists, is probably due to the fact that they have not in the past been thought qualified to express any views worth listening to; and indeed, as they for so long were less well educated, had less experience and less knowledge, and possibly narrower lives, they were not in fact able to talk as well as men could. So a conversation even now may run on the lines of the men condescending to the women, explaining everything to them from the height of their better knowledge, while the women "play up to" the men—and even go so far sometimes as to pretend they are ignorant, more in need of instruction than they are in fact. Though it may be remarked here that men do not really like a "silly" woman, and more and more men, especially young men, do like a woman or girl to be able to talk sensibly and to be interesting as well as interested.

Occasionally girls are told that if they want to please a man all they have to do is to get him started talking about his work and himself, and that all that is then necessary is to listen as intelligently and amiably as possible. That is very doubtful. In the past, when women had no careers of their own, the man's career did give an easy subject, but men on the whole expect more from women now. If the woman does let the talk centre round the man's work and interests, that attitude will not produce the best results. The conversation will be too "one-sided." In order to achieve the most interesting and exciting talks, both parties must be honest in expressing their views and tastes and each must give and take. The men must be really wishful to hear what the women think, and the women must be prepared to give their contribution. It is necessary to find subjects in which both are interested, and nowadays women are more on an equality in what they do, their work and their lives are more varied, and so are their interests and activities. Each must set out to find what they *both* enjoy talking about. It may be politics, or books, or walking, or acting —anything which is shared by both sexes.

It is never safe to generalize, but perhaps one might venture to say that on the whole women are a little more able to talk lightly and to begin a conversation than men, because women do not, quite so often, suffer from awkwardness, do not so often feel "tongue-tied." Men quite often are stiff and slow in beginning a conversation, and are aware of this and that makes them worse. Women can smile and chatter and that is accepted, but a man cannot. What is the man to do? Clearly not grin and gabble! If a man does take things more seriously he must not go against his character and try to be light or bright. He will have to screw himself up not to be quite tongue-tied, but he can do a good deal in the way of trying not to be slow, not to be too hesitating. He can try to answer up and be as prompt as he can. Practice here does gradually wear off that "roughness" and make him able to get going and keep going. He might perhaps cheer himself by reflecting that the woman or girl who rushes gaily ahead sometimes is suffering from the opposite form of shyness. She talks too much and too quickly because she is shy, and dare not stop to think. Later on she may be wishing she could learn not to talk a lot of rubbish, but to be rather slower and think a little more before she begins chattering away.

If we want good conversation in mixed company we might perhaps take a few things which ought to be avoided. On the men's side, they should realize that accounts of sporting feats they have achieved or a detailed account of their work may not be deeply exciting to a woman—who, unless a near relation, is not going to be thrilled with a man's talk of athletics, or his daily routine. Men are too innocently unaware of how a woman's heart may sink when a man's talk begins: "I had a splendid day today, I must tell you about it! . . ."

Women in their turn create absolute havoc in conversation by their truly fatal tendency to talk about their families, especially their children. One knows the woman who will begin any conversation: "I must tell you what baby did today, he really is marvellous. He climbed on a chair and reached himself an apple off the table and, what do you think, he ate every bit, skin and all, and he's none the worse," and so on. Well, the baby's father will, quite rightly, be thrilled to hear of his son's enterprise and health. But other people will not be so interested, or if they are in the first piece of news they will cease to be, if the proud mother goes on to further deeds, or to what all the other children may be doing. In a sense this parental pride, and the belief that what is deeply interesting to the mother will be equally entrancing to all and sundry, is both human and rather touching. But, carried to excess, as it too often is, it makes conversation hopeless. Kind friends, who are interested in the family, will always inquire after its members, and be glad to hear of their doings, but even the kindest and most sympathetic will want to talk of other things as well, and less kindly people will end by saying: "She's dull, she never talks of anything but her family and her own affairs." Few people will honestly want to hear a long account of a child's progress, either its health or its school, or its achievements at games, or even its progress in life, marriage, etc. (And we may rather unkindly notice that a woman who talks so much about her family often takes no interest at all in anyone else's.) One may listen to this torrent of family details and try to be interested, but secretly one will be in a frenzy of irritation. Women are sometimes so dense in this respect that if a new acquaintance merely asks: "And have you any children?" a long detailed description of son, daughter, perhaps brother and sister, bursts out; yet who can really be deeply interested in persons they have never seen? Women had better make a rule: "I must not talk too much about my family, people are not as interested in them as all that."

One difficulty is, women may feel that they should not try to talk about serious subjects, or seem "too clever." They have something left of the old idea that men do not like clever women. Well, no one likes a woman who tries to show she is clever, or who is terribly "earnest" about everything. But men do like women—and girls—to talk sense.

It is true that women can give a great contribution to conversation by the fact that they are not expected always to be "serious" or deal with rather "deep" points.

They can and do bring their own special gift to bear. They can give to conversation lightness and sparkle. If men do not perhaps take women's views so very seriously, yet they certainly enjoy the light touch, the gaiety, almost the "frivolity" of women. Men cannot usually supply that sparkle, but they can appreciate it. Certainly if talk is getting rather "heavy" it is a woman who can usually brighten it all up by some cheerful, almost absurd remark. Indeed, a woman may have to be truly unselfish here, and risk making a fool of herself. She will have the consolation of knowing that she has removed a "block" in conversation, and that, after all, her light-hearted absurdity will not be severely judged. Both parties will gain if they keep in mind the points we have mentioned above. Men must not be too "superior," women must not be too "silly," men must not lay down the law, women must not talk too much of home and family. Both ought to think of their conversation as a meeting-place for men and women to learn each other's ideas, and, where there is the added interest and amusement of being in "mixed company," not just with one's own sex.

Let us come out into the open. Men and women do enjoy, of course, meeting and talking. Granted that men possibly think they "talk more sense," and inwardly think women's talk is amusing, but not very "deep" or to be taken too seriously, still they find it refreshing. Women for their part do get pleasure from hearing a man talk well and perhaps make things which they have not understood clear to them. Then we want to go further and find out how we can get a good level of mixed conversation, get the best out of it in fact. Well, clearly both must wish to hear the other's point of view, and be prepared to be reasonable and sympathetic where they do not agree. (Naturally, as men and women do agree on many matters, we need not consider that aspect.) It is often really a help for one to say: "Well, that's the man's point of view"—say on such a subject as the management and control of the family finances—and then let the woman say: "Yes, I see all that, but as a woman this is what I think. . . ."

One rather odd little instance may illustrate this. A man and a woman were talking about soldiering as a profession, the man being a regular soldier. The woman said, what she felt, that it must be terrible to have a profession which aimed at—or resulted in—killing other human beings. The man gave his view, which was that he looked on himself as a protector, trained to preserve the lives of others. Each looked at the matter from quite different points of view, but as a result of their conversation each understood the other. These differences, due to many causes, should not be a hindrance, they should be a help to conversation, for each party brings its own gifts, as we may call them. If men may be more "fair-minded," better able to form a sound opinion (even, dare one say, more "generous," less "catty" in their judgments?), yet women may be more sympathetic and have more insight into other people's difficulties. That is, of course, arguable. What is quite certain is that if each tries to make his conversation interesting to the other, if each tries honestly to understand the other, and if each uses his or her own experiences as man or woman, the result will be enjoyable and interesting. We may decide after such talk that there can be no doubt conversation between men and women has a variety which can give the greatest possible pleasure.

CHAPTER TEN

WOMEN TALKING TOGETHER

"I said to her . . . and she said to me" — too usual in all sections — a special need for women to improve conversation amongst themselves — unfortunate low level — usual topics — home life, children, meals, clothes. To be avoided — gossip — its pleasures and its evils — part played by talk about what are women's normal interests — need for women to refresh themselves by talk on more general subjects — points of wider interest which do improve women's conversations — public work — wider reading — women's clubs and institutes — gradual equality and spread of education — the new generation — summary, women's conversation, often too narrow but need for wider and better talk really often felt.

WOMEN, talking together, it must perhaps regretfully be said, only too often have a low level of conversation. To begin with, they seem to have a fatal habit of "direct narration." Listen to two women talking, on a bus or in a shop or having a meal together. Too often there comes the repeated: "I said to her . . ." and then "she said to me . . ." "Well, I said . . . and what do you think she said! I said. . . ." That tells a tale in itself. Women do so much tend simply to repeat talks they have had. In other words they are, though they may not know it, gossiping. That is not conversation, and it really means women do not gain enough by such talks. When they are not indulging in these repetitions of what has been said, when they really try to talk to other women, then again, regretfully, one knows that too often the talk is about children, meals, clothes, in fact small talk about domestic life.

Granted, of course, that women love to talk about these subjects, they are the stuff of life. They are the normal interests of the normal woman and so, of course, she will want to talk about them and be glad to exchange her views and experiences with other women who share them. No one should deny the pleasure women get from talking about clothes, or object to it, for after all a woman's appearance is of great importance. If she looks becomingly dressed, not only is she happy but nice clothes do brighten up the whole world, for everyone enjoys seeing someone who is well turned-out. In the same way it is natural that women should want to talk about their homes, their cooking, their curtains and carpets, for the home depends on the woman's taste.

Of course she will want to talk about her children, perhaps discuss her difficulties, ask about education and so on. Women like to give advice, and some like being given it, so women's talk will always contain a large slice of family matters. There is nothing to be ashamed of in all this, but at the same time women should realize that by dwelling on those subjects they do not get enough change and refreshment. Conversation ought really to give pleasure by giving new ideas, and "domestic" talk does not do that. The ideal is to come away from a talk feeling: "I really did enjoy that, it was so interesting."

Worse than feeling that perhaps after all the talk has been dull, is the guilty feeling that perhaps one has gossiped, and not always kindly. It has to be faced, women are often accused of being "cats," just because when they meet they do often criticize other women. This is an old story. More than a hundred years ago Jane Taylor gave the best example of what passed then as women's conversation:

"Out the scandal came at last
'Come, then, I'll tell you something more'
Says she—'Eliza shut the door—
I would not trust a creature here
For all the world but you, my dear.
Perhaps it's false—I wish it may,
But let it go no further, pray!'

"And how we did enjoy the sport!
And echo every faint report,
And answer every candid doubt,
And turn her motives inside out,
And holes in all her virtue pick,
Till we were sated, almost sick."

Well, perhaps things are not as bad as that now! But women do still often begin a talk by saying: "Now, tell me all the gossip." It may be good-natured and indeed is generally perfectly harmless and amusing and it does represent women's real keen interest in human beings as opposed to abstract things such as politics. Yet it does not, at its best, help very much, and it may lead to regrets. La Rochefoucauld said (and as it happens he was speaking to men): "Never say anything you may regret later"; a truly golden rule.

Women often do not realize what they miss by keeping to narrow topics. The woman whose life is taken up by caring for her home and her family does grow "stale" from lack of variety and change. She needs something to take her out of herself. If when she meets other women she can talk about general subjects she would find that a refreshment. She would take new ideas back with her to her home. If women have met together and perhaps unexpectedly the talk has turned on wider subjects, books or politics, or problems which are being discussed today such as the laws on marriage and divorce, or child delinquents, quite often afterwards those people will say or think to themselves: "Well, that was a nice talk, I feel quite freshened up by it."

Sometimes women may be nervous about starting conversation on such subjects. They may have to begin on simpler lines, talk about the radio programmes or the film at the local cinema. But they ought to make a real effort to talk about things, not people. Actually, nowadays women do have more subjects to talk about. Many are engaged in public work, most places now have women on local councils, or women J.P.s. Those who do not themselves occupy such posts can discuss whether they will vote for a woman or even whether they approve of women as jurors, J.P.s and M.P.s. Women's clubs and institutes give many things to talk about. Women and girls belong to clubs, and to drama societies and choral societies. They can find plenty to talk about there. It is interesting to talk about all these activities. Again, it cannot be sufficiently impressed that at these clubs and meetings and societies if the members only talk gossip or trivialities they lose half their advantages. Women need to get away from details and personalities. If one or two will only start talking about a general subject the others will take it up. As one woman said about a class she was attending on home-dressmaking: "I like going to it because often some of them talk about books and things I don't hear about in my own home."

It is to be expected, indeed, that as education and general opportunities develop women's interests will develop, too. The young generation today does in some respects appear to have profited by modern advantages.

Girls do go to work and to interesting work. They do have more interesting holidays certainly than did their grandmothers. They do go to cinemas and theatres and (as statistics show) they do read more books. So let us hope they will learn to profit by all this and talk about the outside world.

Women may largely be unaware of what they could do, and how much they could gain, if they would make resolutions every time they were going to meet other women, and inwardly resolve to try to "keep off" gossip and personalities and talk about their families, if they were to make up their minds to try to talk about something else, in which others may be interested, and try to discuss something they have read in the paper, or some play or film or book which other people are talking or writing about. Many would be greatly surprised to find how much more enjoyable their conversations become. Men enjoy "sensible" talks, and women do, too. If they made these efforts, and if they were not secretly ashamed and almost embarrassed at the idea of setting out with a plan to talk about interesting things, they would soon find the truth. After all, women are neither more stupid, more silly, nor more dull than men, and there is no reason why their conversation should be so. They ought to be ashamed if it is. Women must really try to improve their conversational powers, but it may be a case of saying: "If at first you don't succeed, try, try, try again." It is no good waiting for someone else to take the lead, each woman must be ready to begin on a subject of conversation. Nor is it fair to let others do all the talking, and have no help given to them.

One reason—or excuse—can be put forward. Women whose days are very largely passed in their own homes do too often find themselves living rather narrow lives. Girls today who give up their work when they marry and devote themselves to running a home for their husbands and children are often conscious that they are losing hold on their interests, they have no time to read or to go out. They spend most of their time alone indoors, and this often makes them a little sad and regretful. They want to run their homes and are perfectly willing to face the sacrifices this may involve, but at the back of their minds lurks the idea they may be becoming "dull," and in the end may be less good companions to their husbands and less interesting mothers to their children. When they do go out and meet others they will say: "Oh! I just am so busy at home, I can't keep up with things," and unfortunately too often their conversation with their friends does turn on details of domestic life. It is a problem that has to be faced. How can the housewife, middle-aged or young, keep herself from having nothing but home affairs to talk about? Well, first, she should really try, when she is talking to other people, to keep off these topics. Naturally she will want to chat a little about these absorbing points. Is it economical to have a washing-machine? Are pressure cookers useful for small families? What shops are best for certain things? All these are, up to a point, of great interest to any housewife. If she is meeting her friend for a cup of coffee or tea she could again make up her mind: "I must get away from this eternal talk about housekeeping." If she can only remember she can force herself to take some other topic to talk over. If she has had time to look at a paper she can decide she will ask her friend what she thinks on the main topic in the newspaper that day. Or she can again make a rule she will try to listen to the radio and find something there which will take her friend right away from the cooking stove or the sink.

When, as often happens, these housewives meet together with their husbands and the two families spend an evening together, the thing to aim at is not to let the men talk on whatever they are keen about, while the two wives discuss their home problems. That again keeps the women in the same old rut, and the men, though they may not realize it, are taking for granted that the women want to talk about their homes while the men will talk about something slightly more interesting. Probably here it is the women who ought to take the initiative. They ought, firmly if they can, to join in the men's talk. Or they can say: "Now you two have gone on long enough about that, we want to hear what you think about something else!" Men and women today do quite naturally share an interest in all sorts of outside things. For instance, development of housing, or road safety, very often plain "politics," or local political concerns. Everyone will enjoy the evening more if all have tried to talk over some outside thing. After all, too, we do not any longer live in Victorian times, when a woman was not expected to discuss or argue or even be interested in politics or literature and so on.

Women have nowadays received a better education, they are citizens, and they can and should expect the men to consider their views worth hearing. They need not feel themselves less able to talk than the men. Naturally, no woman or girl wants to get the reputation of always asserting herself, or talking about a subject of which she knows nothing, but at the same time women are quite often too shy, let themselves think they cannot talk about anything but their own province of home affairs, and so they sit silent and end by actually not being able to enter into talk on other subjects. If they cannot possibly take an interest in anything outside, well, sad as that is and really blameworthy, then they can at least make an effort to talk of the more interesting side of home life—say, the "doing up" of a room, the advantages or disadvantages of distemper or wallpaper, the best colours for rooms which get little sun, or home carpentering, or what can be planned in the garden. The men can be interested in and talk about such topics. Though, as has been said, it will be so much better for everyone if the women will make efforts to be more alert, and in the course of the day put away in a corner of their minds outside topics which they could talk about later on.

Sometimes, too, it is the woman who is the reader, or the gardener. The man will say: "My wife's keen on books, I don't read much myself," or: "She's the gardener and I leave all that to her." Then it is up to the woman to find something she can discuss with the men, tell them what she has just read and ask what they think. However, one and all will enjoy conversation which is something more than chat about persons, and which distracts one's thoughts from "the daily round," by being real conversation about ideas and outside events.

CHAPTER ELEVEN

TALKING TO PEOPLE IN TROUBLE

*Conversation with people who are ill or in trouble —
cheerful conversation with those who are ill — family
news — need to give sick people something fresh to
think about and to leave them with new ideas to
meditate about after the visit — what to avoid — recital
of depressing news — of trivialities — essential to divert
thoughts of sick people into fresh channels — same
applies to those in trouble — sympathy — but need to
give fresh ideas — to help people to change their
dwelling on unhappiness — new channels for their
thoughts — unwillingness of those in trouble but will
realize refreshment later. Summary: Leave more cheerful
and leave something to think about after visitor has gone.*

ALWAYS, in this life, we find ourselves sooner or
later faced with visits to be paid to people who
are ill, or who have been overwhelmed by some
great sorrow, perhaps the death of a child or a husband
or wife. It is not always easy to know what to talk about
on these occasions, and much as we may long to be
sympathetic and help our friends these visits may worry
us in advance because we feel embarrassed or shy. We
do not know whether to talk about the illness or the
sorrow, we do not know whether to try to be cheerful,
whether to talk about our own affairs and so on.

If we are going to see someone who is gravely ill,
perhaps facing a long illness, or recovering from a bad
operation, there are some ideas which may make our
visits easier for ourselves and more helpful to our friends.
Naturally, at first one does need to be sympathetic and to
find out how the other person is feeling—are books
needed, or papers to read, or any letters to be written?

Occasionally people arrive to see an invalid and take little or no notice of the patient's health, they do not ask about it but are so full of their own affairs and troubles they set out straight away and pour out all they are full of. Now everyone who is ill dislikes that. After all, they are the sufferers and they do like some interest to be taken in how they are getting on. They also may have grievances and worries which they want to talk about, as anyone who is ill is probably, quite naturally, rather irritable and will be helped if you ask: "Anything bothering you?" If they can have a "good grumble" they will probably feel the better to have talked it all out and will be more amicably disposed after having "got that off my mind." So it is a good idea first to inquire about health, and then about any possible worries.

Then, of course, ill people do like to hear news and gossip about their families and friends in their circle. They like to know if anyone has won a competition—or bought a new frock—or put up a new shed—items of day-to-day news which they miss when they cannot get about. They may enjoy, too, hearing of any parties or meetings, anything which brings to their minds the people they are accustomed to, so that they can feel, however long their illness, they are "keeping in touch."

There is, too, a great deal more we can do for people with long illnesses or much pain to bear, for the whole object of our visits is really to help those who are ill. We really want to do the only thing we can—cheer them up. Well, because of their pain and their loneliness invalids need above all something fresh to think about, something to take them out of themselves. When we have gone away, and they are left alone, they need some fresh idea which they can go on thinking about after we have gone. If they have just been given "chat" and little scraps of news, that will not last them very long, or change the current of their thoughts. It is not, perhaps, very easy, especially if we are going repeatedly to visit them, but it can be done. Of course, different people need different subjects, and we have to think beforehand what particular invalids are at all likely to care about. If we can talk about what is happening in the world they may be able to read more in the papers and look out for what we have talked about. If we have had any interesting experience, we can tell them of it. If we have read any good book, we can talk about it, or offer to lend it and then talk it over on our next visit. We have to be tactful. If we are visiting anyone who is not going to recover we should not talk of our next holiday, or even perhaps of our plans for our garden in the coming year—for he or she may feel that life will have ended by then.

People do exist, however, who can put aside the knowledge that their lives are ending, and who do enjoy talking of the future—other people's futures—as if all were well. Only knowledge of the person concerned will guide us there.

It is clearer to see what to do if we think of the way *not* to talk. We ought to avoid anything that is depressing. So many people go to see someone who is ill and begin at once a catalogue of all that is wrong. It may be eternal complaints over difficulties of food and fuel. It may be grumbles at the disagreeableness of travelling. It may be merely complaints about the weather, but in any case no one who is ill wants to have depressing items talked of, to have grumbles and complaints poured out. In ordinary life no one likes a grumbler and everyone gets depressed if a person is always looking on the gloomy side.

Well, it is far worse for those who are ill, and have enough to feel depressed about themselves without having other people's bothers swamping them. It is quite possible to make up one's mind beforehand: "Now, I must not talk about all these horrid small things," and stick to it. Equally, it is not really a help to give detailed accounts of trivialities—how one was late getting somewhere, how noisy the next-door dog was today, how crowded the café was for "elevenses," and so on and so forth.

Invalids, who may have been looking forward eagerly to a really good talk, will not be very much thrilled with all that. What they will enjoy is if you can really collect beforehand something they can talk about with you, so that they, too, can be roused up to share a talk. Then if you have managed to get on to something which they can continue to think about afterwards you will have been the perfect visitor.

You might try to talk about the time when they will be better, will they feel like having new clothes, or new curtains in their room? Or do they think they would like to try something to amuse them while they are ill—crosswords, jig-saws and so on, and then plan how to get them. Or would they like a plant, to watch it grow? Actually, some of our big hospitals find, for example, how wonderfully the most unlikely patients are amused and interested if they are given a bowl and a couple of gold-fish to watch! Anyway, one can, if one takes the trouble, think of a few things which might open up ideas.

Much of this applies when we go to see anyone who has suffered a great loss. It is always something of an ordeal when we first go to see, or meet, people who have lost someone very dear to them. Probably we have to leave it to them whether we shall speak of their loss. It may be too sad for them even to mention it. They will know we sympathize, and if they want to they themselves will talk of their loss and the dreadful blank they feel. We will want to show our sympathy, but we will also want not to upset them and we just have to wait and see our way there. Apart from that, we have again the same end in view, we want to help them to change the current of their thoughts. We want to do what we can, however little it may be, to give them something fresh, so that they can to some extent get away from their unhappiness and not dwell on it. So, again, we could try to rouse their interest and divert them into thinking of something else.

People who are in great trouble may almost resent this. They may be absorbed in their grief or anxiety, they may want to go on talking it over and may at first dislike any effort to switch them off from it. One woman was nursing her dying husband in a long illness, and a friend, going to see her, after a while said: "Now I am going to talk about outside things; I want to take your mind off." The woman admitted later she had not liked that; she felt she could not be interested in anything other than her husband's illness; but afterwards she realized it had done her good. She always had her sad thoughts, and this friend who just insisted on talking of events going on in the world had really given her refreshment and she was the better for it.

In fact, to sum up, all our talks with people who are

ill or in trouble should quite simply aim at making them more cheerful and happier. This is done best of all not by talking of trifles, or of our own bothers, but by trying to give them something they can think about and enjoy going on thinking about after we have gone away.

CHAPTER TWELVE

TALKING TO FOREIGNERS

*In our country — in theirs — things to be avoided —
superiority of our ways — need to try to learn of other
view-points — readiness to accept and try to understand
criticism — finding out others' reactions to national
characteristics — or sport, e.g., bull-fighting — possible
subjects leading to real discussion — class structure —
houses and homes — furniture — hot and cold in
climate and in homes — education of children — differences in behaviour to foreigners — better results in conversation if ask not what they admire but what they
dislike.*

DURING the last war very many foreigners came
to Britain, people from every part of the world,
and so there were more opportunities than ever
before of talking to them. Now when foreigners come
there are certain ways of talking to them which will
annoy them, though they may be too polite to say so.
As many still come as tourists or on business, it is worth
while just giving a little thought to them. First and
foremost there is the need not to talk from a "superior"
point of view. We may think our way of doing things—
regulating our traffic and having the rule of right-hand
drive, or the arrangement of our shop windows, or the
kind of shoes we wear—is the best, but we simply ought
not to say so. The foreigner will not like it, and above
and beyond that it is not in the least interesting to him
to hear our ideas. He sees for himself what are our ways
of doing things and he can decide for himself if he
prefers them or his own.

All this holds good if we ourselves go abroad. We shall

meet foreigners in trains, motor-coaches, restaurants and hotels. Our travelling will be far more interesting if we try to talk to the people of the country. Very many can speak some English and they are delighted to try, only unfortunately they find from experience English people are not very ready to talk. Usually this is shyness, but the foreigner thinks it part of our stand-offish, almost rude ways. Once you begin to talk you usually find the greatest friendliness. A foreigner will be delighted if you ask him about the countryside as you pass through it. Or if you ask what will be the nicest thing to choose on a menu. (Only do not bore them by complaints of how much better their food is nowadays than ours! They have heard quite enough about that.) They will love giving you advice, and be anxious you should not miss anything of which they are proud. They will *not* want to be told that "we do things differently." They do not care if we do, and they will take it as criticism of their way of life.

We shall really enjoy talking to a foreigner far more if we do not set out to talk of our ways or our views, but ask him about his own. He will be far more likely to interest us, too, if instead of saying (as practically everyone does): "How do you like our country?" one says instead: "Now, what do you dislike over here?" He will probably be delighted to say what he finds odd or less to his liking than what he has at home. Then we can talk about it. Ask why does he do things differently and explain why we have our way. One small instance: foreign newspapers are small in size compared to ours; or, as another example, almost all Continental countries have cafés with tables and chairs on the pavement, even where the climate is not much different from ours, and,

of course, almost all drink coffee and not tea. Well, ask
a foreigner what he thinks about our papers, or cafés, or
beverages! Then you must be ready to accept his
criticisms. It is hopeless, of course, to get cross, or just
to say: "Oh, well, we don't like that sort of thing." You
have to be firm with yourself. Remember, our ways are
very different, but it does not follow they are the best or
nicest; we might gain from their ideas. (As, for example,
places in England are beginning to put up coloured
umbrellas and tables outside hotels and cafés.) We have
to accept criticism in a cheerful, friendly way, and go on
to try to understand what is the other point of view.

Again, if it is possible to do it without ending in a
quarrel, it is always interesting to find out what others
think of us as a nation. Many foreigners have the idea
that we are stiff, unfriendly, disagreeable, and they are
surprised and delighted when they come over here to
find this is not so. So often one now reads letters in the
newspapers saying: "I was struck most of all by the
friendliness." Perhaps the war improved us there, when
we tried to welcome those who came as refugees or
allies, but it does seem as if our national character had
improved in this respect, and in any case a foreigner will
love to tell us how he finds us. We can compare ourselves
with his countrymen and learn a good deal. For example,
a visiting Italian said that one thing which amazed him
was the way the English were always laughing. Italians
apparently smile, but do not laugh; and certainly, when
one thinks, there is a good deal of laughter in our cafés
or pubs or in the streets. A kind foreigner will praise us,
but you will get far more interest if you ask him what
he does not like, or what improvements he would
suggest!

Foreigners are often interested to talk about our "sports." Today almost all nations are international with regard to football, which is played everywhere, and, to a much less extent, cricket. But they like to tell one about their own national sports. Here we terribly often vex and annoy by our belief "we know best"; the most obvious instance being the bull-fights of Spain. Spaniards will bitterly resent our condemning this out of hand as cruel. They will really think we cannot judge, as most of us have never seen a bull-fight. We certainly do not understand the Spanish point of view—and he will condemn us as "hypocrites" because he considers our fox-hunting just as cruel, and probably thinks it worse because it is not a national spectacle enjoyed widely by town and country alike. So if we want to discuss this subject with Spaniards we ought to be ready to find out why they enjoy it, or whether they do wish to get rid of it and replace it by, perhaps, football, as some say.

There are so many subjects we can talk about enjoyably if only we start from the idea that we already know our side; what we want to hear is the foreigner's view.

We can have great discussions on politics, only we must *not* insist on the merits of our electoral or parliamentary system. We should ourselves be more interested in finding out what their systems are. For example, anyone from the U.S.A. has no doubt at all his system is better than ours, and comparatively few people here really know what the American system of government is, much less why they think it is more sensible than ours. Sailors are often extremely good at conversations with foreigners, because they do go to other countries and often wish to find out how they are governed. We are possibly so certain our democracy is the best, we do not stop to find out if everyone else agrees, much less the ways in which their forms may be different. Yet here is an excellent topic for conversation.

In a simpler way we can talk, too, about their houses, their homes, their furniture, their meals. Lately we have perhaps come to realize we can learn a lot from other countries on these points. For instance, there is great interest now in the houses of Scandinavia; some people are copying them. We are beginning to have flat roofs and, in cities, roof-gardens. We can discuss these and how far they are suitable or can be adapted to our climate.

We can discuss the way we plan our homes, our kitchens, or our habit of having carpets on our floors where continental people have polished floors and rugs. Many foreign women are horrified at our carpets, they think they are not as clean as their floors and rugs. We can discuss the kind of windows we have, we have sash windows where they prefer lattices, or french windows with shutters. We can, of course, discuss endlessly the advantages and disadvantages of our ways of heating our houses. Here, if we are talking to Americans, we know in advance we are the ones who will be criticized for our lack of "central heating" and of our relatively cold rooms, and we can be prepared to stand up for our ways if we feel like it. (We can say we think it healthier, or that central heating spoils furniture and so on.)

Everyone enjoys talking about these domestic matters, for they are the essentials in everyone's lives. Food is not usually as agreeable a topic because, quite apart from our present difficulties, tastes do seem to be fundamentally different here, and we generally feel that though other countries have great merits in some of their ideas on cooking, on the whole we like our own.

We can find a great deal to talk about in education and the upbringing of children and young people. We can discuss the level of education, the best age for beginning school, the kind of schools or colleges each country has, whether boys and girls should go to mixed schools, even the part played by religious teaching, and so on.

In fact, once you get on to children and young people you never lack for talk. Foreigners, after all, do have many of the same interests as ourselves. One radio programme with accounts of a town abroad described how all over Europe men and women were talking about one and the same problems. Peace and war, of course; then housing, then prices and wages. In every country they talked, too, of the growth of crime amongst young people, and its causes, and how to meet the problem. They talked of the bad results on any nation of such things as drunkenness and gambling and of the problems of easy divorce. If people are alike interested in these things we can be sure, too, they will be interested in the same way as we ourselves are in travelling, holidays, scenery, furniture and national taste in food, or in the ways of modern young people.

If we are really to enjoy meeting foreigners, and if they are to enjoy meeting us, then we have to collect ourselves and be firm that what will give the best results is to let them give their views. Try to draw out what they think. Do not just explain, or praise, our ways. Be reasonable, and bear in mind they will not like some of our habits and ideas, that to many we are a strange and by reputation not a very friendly or agreeable people, that we are thought to be proud, pleased with ourselves and rather rude and overbearing. Well, we can ask them whether they think so, and if, having met us, they still think so. And if so, why. At least then we shall have a lively conversation, and one which both parties may enjoy very much, and as a result be all the better friends.

CHAPTER THIRTEEN

CONVERSATION BETWEEN YOUNG AND OLD

What the young do not like from the old — advice and comparisons with past — criticism — lack of sympathy with changed ideas and conditions — what to aim at — tolerance — learn their view — do not press our views — example: Brains Trust where old asked young their views — talking to the old — patience — love of old to recall past — do not worry or startle with new ideas — sympathy and affection — enjoyment of old and young in joint conversation — may be rare — depends chiefly on attitude of old — young must not be bored — amiable comparisons — let young decide what they wish to talk about — no impatience on either side — interest from variety of experience on both sides.

POSSIBLY young people do not care about talking to older people; that has to be faced at the outset. Yet in any family group the young people will of necessity often have to talk to their elders. Sometimes, too, young people will say they do enjoy talking with those who are older, because to them the gulf between different age groups gives variety and interest. Here is a clue. Young people may enjoy hearing of the experiences of an older generation, they may be fascinated by the differences in upbringing, in general behaviour, in tastes; to them the stories of the world as it was twenty or thirty years ago may have an amusing, almost a romantic character. But one thing is to be noticed here, the young do not want comparisons of the past and present, almost invariably to the disadvantage of the young people today. How irritated they get and how bored when they hear the phrase: "Young people didn't do that when I was young," or: "In my young days we weren't supposed to do this, that or the other." In the first place, everyone, young or old, knows how very much things have changed in the last twenty or thirty years, they know that young people have more liberty, are more free-and-easy in every way. As the young people have grown up in this new atmosphere, that to them is the world as they know it. They have not the slightest wish to return to bygone days and ways—nor are they in any degree likely to think those ways were better than their own. They resent, too, the idea that the older generation were really "better behaved," it offends them to have their ways "run down," and criticism of this sort will make them irritated and annoyed at the assumption the older people were so much better. Besides, if we did but know it, every generation has said exactly the same. Even in the days of Queen Elizabeth parents deplored the bad manners and general deterioration of the young, and again and again in diaries, memoirs and novels you will find this same old story—the young do not behave as nicely as the older generation did when they were young. In short, the young do not like criticism from people who they feel are not really able to judge. They may say, and will certainly think: "But things are different now," and they may think, too, that life was easier for their elders and that the real difficulties and troubles of the young generation cannot be fully understood by the older.

In the same category, and connected with criticism, is advice. Generally it is not wished for or asked for, but again and again the older generation will say: "Well, if I were you I shouldn't dream of doing that," or: "Don't you think that's a very stupid way to behave, now *I*

should do this. . . ." On the whole young people are
very polite and restrained on these occasions. They do
not burst out: "But I didn't ask for your opinion," or:
"But I'm *not* you and so I shan't dream of doing as you
would," though if sorely tried they will inwardly be
saying it to themselves. If a young person really and
truly values the older person's opinion he or she will ask
for it. But in general, however kindly meant or expressed,
the advice of older people is not welcomed; and even if
the young persons may in their hearts feel that the
advice is good, a sort of natural contrariness makes them
react against it. Deep down, possibly, this is due to the
fact that younger people, just because they are young,
do not quite believe the older people can truly understand and sympathize. They feel the differences are so
great, and time has flown by and the older people simply
do not live in the same world and cannot understand.

A further difficulty is that most young people have a
kind of shyness, or embarrassment, in talking about
serious subjects with their elders. They do not in the
least mind talking over difficulties and problems with
their own generation. But in a way that is difficult to
define they feel that they just don't want to talk even
to their parents on some subjects. It has nothing whatever to do with affection, much less the fear of being
"found fault with" or of "shocking" their parents by
their views. In many families where there is the deepest
affection and real sympathy and tolerance from the
parents there is still this barrier raised by the young.
Quite a common example is religion—sometimes problems such as marriage or divorce, sometimes just political
views. It may be the natural desire of the young to have
their independence, they want to keep part of their

thoughts and ideas to themselves. It may be the equally natural inclination of youth to "rebel"—though that is too strong a word really—against the accepted old-fashioned view, but this instinct does exist. Often young people will say: "I can't bear it when Mum or Dad tries to talk to me about religion," or whatever it is. Even the most devoted parents and children may experience this. So for the older generation the safe rule is: do not try to begin on these subjects, let the conversation start by the younger, if they wish, asking: "What do you really think about this?"

If old and young are discussing matters, or talking together, the tolerance must come from the older person. They may be inclined to speak from the height of their greater experience. "My dear child, you do not really know what you're talking about," or: "You don't know enough to form an opinion." That is calculated to make any young person bristle up. They will think "experience" is not everything. "I have a right to my own ideas." Probably what they want is the chance to express their opinions, to try them out to see how the argument looks when put into words. They will be vexed and hurt if their efforts to think for themselves are rather crushed by the older generation's wider experience. It does call for tolerance and tact, for the young may seem too self-assured, too crude. It is possible, however, to say: "Well now, why do you think that?" or: "What do you think would happen if your ideas were put into practice?" or: "What makes you think that, what have you seen or read or heard that convinces you?"

Older people will help most in truly honest conversations if they will try to reverse the usual rule; if they will try first to get the young to give their views, and say why they hold them, and do not press their own. The young probably think they know in advance what their elders will think—"Of course, I know you won't agree, you'll say you weren't brought up like that." They think they can tell what views their relations are likely to have, and what they are struggling to do is to get their own ideas clear, and they may want to get them clear by contrasting them with what older people think. For example, a girl may want to leave home, possibly leaving a mother or father alone with no other members of the family to be with them. She may want to talk this over with an aunt, but she perhaps does not so much want the aunt to advise her, she wants to get clear and in the open her own idea of what it is right for her to do. Or a boy may dislike the career his father has planned, he wants to strike out into something quite different. If he talks to an uncle, it is no sort of help to be told: "Well, I would never have gone against my father's wishes, I'd have known he knew what was the most sensible thing for me to do." The boy and girl feel *their* case is different, what someone else would have done years ago may not help in the least in deciding what should be done now. So let the elders aim most at finding out just why the young people wish to take a course of action, and let them try to remember that the experience of the past may not be what will help the present. Look at the problem simply from the view-point of present-day conditions and ideas.

It always comes back to this: The older generation must pay a great deal of attention to and give a great deal of weight to the views of the young, and try to think less of the importance of their own views. A very good example of this came up in a radio programme, a sort of "Brains Trust" on religious matters, between a team of older people and a young audience. At first the younger people asked questions, and the team of older people answered them, with all the knowledge and experience they had. Then a change was made, and the older team put questions to the young: "What do you think of these problems?" (One was whether it is wrong not to pay a bus or train fare if the conductor is not there to receive it.) It was extraordinarily interesting to hear the young people give their views (and one was struck by their modesty in giving them), ånd it gave the impression the young people would be helped and strengthened by the realization their views were of value and of interest to their elders. That seems the right and most helpful attitude, and, after all, older people do wish most earnestly to help the young—and not to bore and irritate them, or leave them feeling blank. The young people, on their side, have to be patient, especially when talking to much older people. It is often very boring to listen to old people talking of the past, often repeating themselves, often telling the same thing over and over.

The surest way for the young to keep cheerful and good-tempered in these circumstances is if they can keep on saying to themselves: "This is just old age. They're old, they can't help it." For, indeed, old age is a physical thing and the old people's minds and memories are changing and are beyond their control. It gives the old so much pleasure—perhaps the only pleasure they get from conversation—if they can go on recalling the past, and they simply cannot help repeating themselves. So do not let young people interrupt: "But you've told us that before," or: "Why, you've just been saying all that." Let them try, however hard it may be, to listen, and listen as if they had *not* heard it all before, and console themselves by the knowledge this is just the one thing they can do to give the old people a little enjoyment.

Another thing, though less common, is that old people are sometimes startled and upset if the young insist on putting forth very bold and startling ideas. Very old people cannot stand shocks of any kind; a talk which startles and vexes them really upsets them very much. Old age needs to be treated gently in words as well as in deeds.

Almost all these difficulties are safely overcome just by affection and sympathy. That is true for both sides. Older people who are truly sympathetic will not hurt the feelings of the young, either by snubbing them or laughing at their ideas or showing that they are not very much impressed by them. They will just listen and be kind. The young, in the same way, if they really feel warm affection for the old, will quite naturally avoid talking so as to hurt or upset. So the problems are solved.

In a wider sense, when young people are talking not to relations but just to older people they know, there may, perhaps, be a sense of more freedom, since neither side has to consider "affection" and the fear of hurt feelings. More can be said, and more light-heartedly, because it does not matter so much; the talkers are not members of the same family, and things said will not be thought about and brooded over, and it often is a "change" for the young. They do sometimes get a little tired of the conversation of their own age group. They may not express it, or be quite aware of it, but every now and then they will find they quite enjoy talking to older people. It may be rather rare, but still boys or girls may very much enjoy a talk with someone older, and may even feel it helps them, makes them more mature. Only the older person must always be sure he does not patronize, and he must not bore the young. It is the older person who must be prepared to let the young decide what they want to talk about, unless the younger one is shy and needs encouragement to "get going." Both parties will have to grasp the idea that it is fatal to be impatient. Both will, perhaps, have to listen to what they do not agree with. The thing to do is to listen and then to argue, and if both sides really want to exchange ideas, and to compare experiences, each respecting the other, then a great deal of pleasure and happiness can follow. Older people almost always love talking to the young. They want to keep in touch with the new world, they want to know how the new generation is getting along; they do not want to feel, because they are old, they are "out of it all." Perhaps they must take pains to get the young to wish to talk to them, but if they truly show sympathy and interest they will probably have their reward and the young will like to pour out their ideas and explain all they think and hope for in the world of the new generation.

CHAPTER FOURTEEN

CASUAL CONVERSATIONS

*Conversations on journeys — should one talk in trains? —
if so, when? — possible openings — and subjects —
what one gains by such conversations — better results
sometimes if occupation not known — the university
professor who pretended to be a commercial traveller —
glimpses into other people's lives — interest from strangers' different experiences. Conversation on holidays —
in hotels — in motor-coaches — on expeditions.*

ACCORDING to old-fashioned ideas one "ought not
to enter into conversation with strangers." Like so
many former conventions, this has largely been
swept away now, and we can, and often do, talk to com-
plete strangers whom we meet casually. The commonest
occasion is on a journey. Of course, many people heartily
dislike talking in trains. If one is tired or wants to read
in peace, people who will talk to each other, or worse
still, will try to talk to you, are the most awful form
of nuisance. Some people deeply enjoy, too, the feeling
that, once settled down in a railway carriage, there is
no need whatever, in England at any rate, for one word
to be exchanged, and four people may travel from
London to Plymouth without a syllable passing their
lips, and yet this is considered neither rude nor strange.

Granted all that, there is still the other side. It is often
most interesting to talk to people on a journey. For one
thing, the chances are they will be people with quite
different work or lives from our own, and people we
would not ordinarily come across. So the train-traveller
may find himself in a carriage with two countrymen and
they will tend to talk of country life, the work on a

farm and so on, all of which is unfamiliar to him. For example, a man travelling to the West Country found himself in company with a Canadian airman and two farmers. They got to talking, and the Canadian, who in his own country was also a farmer, could describe the effects on the soil of using a new plough which was only just being introduced into England and which the Canadian thought would not suit our conditions. A more fantastic case was a teacher who, travelling during the war in a compartment full of airmen, found she came from the same part of England as two of the men, and they ended by reciting to her old spells—white witch-craft—which they both knew, and could say had been used by their grandparents. Such odd little romantic scraps do crop up, and there is a fascination from hearing such talk.

Openings to conversation have to come of themselves. No one is more tiresome than the talkative person who insists on conversation when clearly everyone else wants to be quiet, and worst of all is the person who, however deep one may be in a book, quite deliberately interrupts and insists on comments on the weather, or the country-side, or the train's shortcomings, and makes that a prelude for rambling talk on anything. So, clearly, the first thing is for people, usually on a long journey, to show they want some change from reading or silence, only always *both* should be ready to enjoy a talk, not just one of them. It is a way of passing the time, and one may be amused and interested at hearing what other people know when their lives are in all probability quite different from our own.

One of the fascinating things is to look at the books or papers other people are reading. You can tell very often who are real readers; they may have a book from a library, or they may have a book which is up to date and being talked out. Or, more rarely, they may have a "learned" book, perhaps history or travels. If one has not read it, and a chance comes when they lay down the book, you can ask them what it is like, are they finding it good? Or, if you have read it, you can ask their opinion and compare notes. Readers can generally find such talk easy and interesting, and especially so because with friends one knows their tastes and can guess what they will think; with a stranger one simply has no idea and it is amusing to find out.

Again, perhaps apologetically, one must say that if one has been travelling with children, and they get out at some station, those who are left will most often express relief. More rarely they may praise the good behaviour of the departed little passengers. But so often this opening can, and does, lead to a discussion of the way children should behave, whether it is unreasonable to expect them to be quiet, whether they should have special compartments to themselves, and so on.

Sometimes just casual talk about the places through which the train is running may give an opening. If you enter London through the dull suburbs and the worse "mean streets," with the grimy little houses backing on to the line, almost certainly you will talk of slums, the need for rebuilding. (You may not be so lucky as one traveller who, going through the eastern approaches and speaking to an old man, was told that he had lived there as a boy when Jack the Ripper was terrorizing the East End.) Or you may notice first the variety of gardens, often so gay and pretty, which mark the "outer-edge," and the pathetic love of flowers and greenery shown in the poorest streets by the boxes and pots which stand on the window-ledges or little flat outhouse roofs, and you can discuss the advantages of the small old-fashioned houses with tiny gardens over the new beautifully built blocks of flats. Talk about flats, gardens and slums clearly can branch out into all sorts of sidelines, and if several people talk you may be sure you will get different views all based on actual experiences and real likes or dislikes.

People from different "income-groups"—if one puts it that way—can really learn a very great deal from these casual conversations, for generally they are people who would never meet and talk in ordinary life, but are thrown together in this way in a train and they can give each other their own special knowledge. Of course, it is quite intolerable if one person is "condescending" and gives himself airs, but luckily such people are not so common nowadays and a genuine friendliness can always be understood at once. People always respond to anyone who is sincere, and who is clearly not in the least thinking himself "different" and people almost always enjoy friendliness and good temper. The traveller who talks only to grumble is, of course, a pest and a bore, and conversation on the lines of nothing but complaints soon becomes utterly dull, and ceases. Indeed, that is almost a rule: do not grumble, it is dull and takes you nowhere.

Sometimes it is far more amusing if people have no idea of the other's occupation. Clearly most people will not talk easily and cheerfully to a traveller whom they find to be very learned; they will be nervous and not like to show their own ignorance and they may feel they themselves and their views could have nothing in common with the other. So an eminent professor used, when travelling, as he frequently did, to put on a cap and make himself look as little like a learned man as he could; sometimes he would go so far as to pose as a commercial traveller, and he declared that as a result, instead of feeling, as he often did, rather cut off from ordinary people, he found himself treated with easy friendliness, as a "good fellow." He liked his fellow men, of all sorts and kinds, and this chance of getting away from his official position gave him pleasure and happiness.

Besides exchanging general talk and ideas, it is also a real widening of one's experience to get even a glimpse of other people's lives. You can travel with people with every sort and kind of work and experience. A woman who is a buyer for a firm, a sailor back from any part of the world, a man who is a glassblower, or a quarryman —clearly if you travel in different parts of the country your opportunities are quite endless and you learn a little of the lives of other people.

Sometimes you may have the less ordinary experience of people who will tell you their sorrows, or their tragedies, finding a sort of relief in telling their stories to strangers whom they will never meet again. If this does come your way, all you have to do is to listen and show sympathy, and all you have to avoid is to try to cap their tale of unhappiness with some similar experience of which you may know. For these people do not want you to talk, they want you to listen so as to give them a relief they cannot perhaps get in their own circle, by pouring out what they are feeling and what they have to bear.

For the lucky people who are able to travel abroad (providing those with whom they may find themselves can speak our language) it is always interesting to hear what the foreigner has to say about his own country.

Here, too, the old rule is true : "To him that has, more shall be given." The person who has interests, who likes to learn about foreign cities and who can compare different countries, will have the best conversations. Those who have little to talk about will not get much in return, for, as usual, people expand and enjoy talking to others who seem "interesting." If you can talk about mountains, and walking, you can get going easily, or if you like seeing castles and picture galleries you can talk about them. If you are interested in other countries' methods of agriculture, or the taxes they pay, you can discuss them, but if you yourself have not considered what you would like to know about foreign ways you will not get very far. After all, you do go abroad to see different countries, and if you can ask about what the people of those countries do and what they admire in their own land you will get what you really set out to obtain, new knowledge, new ideas.

The same applies, in a slightly different way, to holidays spent in your own country. You go away from home, and you want change, variety and something you do not get at home. You will be with different people, either in the place in which you stay, or going on expeditions, or travelling on a coach-tour. What your mind needs is to rub up against other minds. It is no good being "stand-offish," or keeping to yourselves and your own party. You see plenty of each other at home. It will do you far more good and help you much more when your holiday is ended if you have tried to mix with people from other places and other homes. Some may be dull, others noisy, and you may think they are "not your sort." But nine times out of ten you would find that there was a great deal to like, and that just their difference would really give you something fresh. Clearly, then, the thing you must not do is to seem "superior," to show you do not think you will get on very well. If you behave like that you will be left alone. Or if you are shy you may find you do not mix easily. Well, very many people are shy, but if you make an effort people will usually respond.

People always enjoy it, too, if you can be brave and say what you think, especially if you are on an expedition or a tour. You may often find here, for instance, that people are a little shy of saying they want to see a cathedral or a famous old building. They do not want to be thought "serious" or "highbrow." If you really like improving your mind, do not be afraid of saying that you do think such "sights" are interesting, and you can say that after all one can go and look at shops anywhere, but that half the point of going to famous places is to see something celebrated. One may note in passing, too, if you are with a big party, it is often a help in talking afterwards if you make a mental note of something you have specially noticed, a stained-glass window, or a carving, or a picture, or a piece of furniture, so that you can ask the others afterwards if they, too, liked it, or if they did not admire it. Do not just be vague and say: "Well, it was all very nice." Try to have one or two special things you could talk over afterwards. You will probably have a good reward here, for if you can carry out this plan you will find other people who have the same tastes and have liked the same things, and that may lead you on to new friendships.

CHAPTER FIFTEEN

FAMOUS CONVERSATIONS IN BOOKS

Bacon on "Discourse" — Boswell's Johnson — conversations in the Bible — in Shakespeare — lighter conversation in Jane Austen — Charlotte Brontë — Anthony Trollope — fantastic conversations: Alice in Wonderland *— travellers' phrase books — conversation in plays — films — radio.*

IT may not help us in the practical sense, but it may amuse us to see what great writers have thought about conversation. And certain people, too, have come down to us as being celebrated for their talk, such as Dr. Johnson. We can look at some of the conversation written by celebrated authors in their books.

First, here is what Francis Bacon says in his essay "On Discourse": "Some in their discourse desire rather commendation of wit, in being able to hold all arguments . . . some have certain commonplaces and themes wherein they are good, and want variety; which kind of poverty is for the most part tedious, and when it is once perceived, ridiculous. The honourablest part of talk is to give the occasion, and to moderate and pass to somewhat else. . . . It is good in discourse and conversation to vary and intermingle speech of the present occasion with arguments, tales, asking of questions, telling of opinions, and jests, for it is a dull thing to tire, and as we say now to jade anything too far. As for jest, there be certain things which ought to be privileged from it, namely, religion, any man's present business, and any case that deserveth pity, yet there be some that think

their wits have been asleep, except they dart out somewhat that is piquant, that is a vein which would be
bridled. . . . He that questioneth much, shall learn much,
but especially if he apply his questions to the skill of the
persons whom he asketh, for he shall give them occasion
to please themselves in speaking, and himself shall con-
tinually gather knowledge . . . but let him be sure to
leave other men their turn to speak; nay if there be
any that would take up all the time, let him find means
to take them off and bring others on . . . speech of a
man's self ought to be seldom, and well chosen." (Here
the great Elizabethan is putting many of the points we,
too, have considered.)

Now let us look at a few examples of Samuel Johnson's
talk. He is the greatest conversationalist of whom we have
a perfect record, but then he alone had his Boswell to
report faithfully what the great man said. (Johnson himself said he "preferred conversation to books," and he
never wrote his own "table talk.")

Here are a few examples: Boswell (when first intro-
duced to him), "recollecting his prejudice against the
Scotch," said: "Don't tell where I come from!" "From
Scotland," cried Davies roguishly. "Mr. Johnson," said I,
"I do indeed come from Scotland, but I cannot help it."
With that quickness of wit for which he was so remark-
able he seized the expression "come from Scotland" and
as if I had said I had come away from it, retorted:
"That, sir, I find is what a very great many of your
countrymen cannot help."

One day, Johnson, who delighted in his partiality for
Oxford, was talking of the many great men it had produced. Mrs. Piozzi said: "Why, there happens to be no
less than five Cambridge men in the room now." "I did

not," said he, "think of that till you told me; but the wolf don't count the sheep."

Talking of a Quakers' meeting, where Boswell had heard a woman preach, Johnson said: "Sir, a woman preaching is like a dog's walking on his hind legs. It is not done well, but you are surprised to find it done at all." Speaking of sympathy with others: "Sir, it is an affectation to pretend to feel the distress of others as much as they do themselves . . . it is as if one should pretend to feel as much pain while a friend's leg is cutting off as he does." Or, criticizing Mrs. Macauley, when Boswell remarked: "Sir, you have made her ridiculous," Johnson retorted: "That was already done, sir. To endeavour to make her ridiculous is like blacking the chimney." And, when thoroughly bored by a man one day: "He would talk at the club concerning Catiline's conspiracy so I withdrew my attention and thought about Tom Thumb!" Johnson's wife had, he said: "A particular reverence for cleanliness," being like "ladies who become troublesome and sigh for the hour of sweeping their husbands out of the house as dirt"; " 'a clean floor is so comfortable,' she would say, till at last I told her that I thought we had had enough talk about the floor, we would now have a touch at the ceiling."

When people criticized his books he said: "It is better a man should be abused than forgotten." Asked if he objected to flattery, he replied: "What signifies it to protest against flattery? When a person speaks well of one it must be either true or false, you know, if true let us rejoice in his good opinion. If he lies it is a proof he loves more to please me than to sit silent."

Coming to examples of conversation in literature, let us begin with two dialogues taken from the Bible. The first is the beautiful conversation between Naomi and Ruth. Naomi was leaving Moab, where she had gone to live and where her two sons had married Moabite women. The sons are dead and Naomi is returning to her own land. She says to her daughters-in-law: "Go, return each to her mother's house: the Lord deal kindly with you, as ye have dealt with the dead, and with me. The Lord grant that ye may find rest, each of you. . . ." Then she kissed them, and they lifted up their voices and wept. And they said to her : "Surely we will return with thee unto thy people." And Naomi said: "Turn again, my daughters. Why will ye go with me?" and Orpah kissed her mother-in-law, but Ruth clave to her. And Naomi said: "Behold thy sister-in-law is gone back unto her people: return thou after thy sister-in-law." And Ruth said: "Entreat me not to leave thee, or to return from following after thee: for whither thou goest, I will go; and where thou lodgest, I will lodge: thy people shall be my people, and thy God, my God. Where thou diest I will die, and there will I be buried. . . ." So Naomi returned and Ruth her daughter-in-law with her, and they came to Bethlehem in the beginning of the barley harvest.

Or the splendid sarcastic conversation when the Kings of Israel and of Judah are considering whether they shall go to attack the King of Syria. They first consult the "false prophets" of Baal whom Ahab, King of Israel, employs: "And the King said: 'Shall I go up against Ramoth-gilead, or shall I forbear?' And the prophets said: 'Go up, and prosper for the Lord shall deliver it into the hand of the King.'" The King of Judah, however, insists that Micaiah, the true prophet of God, shall also be consulted. "And the King said: 'Micaiah, shall we go up to battle or shall we forbear?' and he answered and said: 'Go and prosper, for the Lord shall deliver it into thy hand.' And the King said to him: 'How many times shall I adjure thee, that thou tell me nothing but what is true in the name of the Lord?' And Micaiah said: 'I saw all Israel scattered upon the hills, like sheep that have no Shepherd,' and the Lord said: 'These have no master, let them return every man to his house in peace.' And the King of Israel said: 'Did I not tell thee that he would prophesy no good, but evil?' . . . and Micaiah said: 'Behold the Lord hath put a lying spirit in the mouth of all these thy prophets.' But Zedekiah (one of the false prophets) went near and smote Micaiah on the cheek and said: 'Which way went the spirit of the Lord from me, to speak to thee?' And Micaiah said: 'Behold thou shalt see in that day, when thou shalt go into an inner chamber to hide thyself.' And the King said: 'Take Micaiah to the governor of the city and say: "Put this fellow in prison and feed him with the bread and water of affliction, until I come in peace."' And Micaiah said: 'If thou return at all in peace, then the Lord hath not spoken by me.'"

If we like now to take examples of conversations from the works of great writers, we may begin with Shakespeare. Of course, there are countless wonderful conversations in his plays (Brutus and Cassius in *Julius Caesar*, Hotspur and his wife in *Henry IV*, etc. Macbeth and Lady Macbeth, etc., etc.). Here we will take only two amongst the most celebrated: In *Hamlet* the gravediggers are talking as they dig Ophelia's grave:

First Clown: Is she to be buried in Christian burial that wilfully seeks her own salvation?

Second Clown: I tell thee she is: and therefore make her grave straight: the crowner hath sat on her and finds it Christian burial.

First Clown: How can that be, unless she drowned herself in her own defence?

Second Clown: Why, 'tis found so.

Second Clown: Will you ha' the truth on't? If this had not been a gentlewoman she should have been buried out of Christian burial.

First Clown: Why, there thou say'st; and the more pity that great folk should have countenance in this world to drown or hang themselves more than their even Christian. Come, my spade. There is no ancient gentlemen but gardeners, ditchers, and grave-makers: They hold up Adam's profession.

Second Clown: Was he a gentleman?

First Clown: He was the first that ever bore arms.

Second Clown: Why he had none.

First Clown: What, art a heathen? How dost thou understand the Scripture? The Scripture says, Adam digged: could he dig without arms? I'll put another question to thee. . . . What is he that builds stronger than either the mason, the shipwright, or the carpenter?

Second Clown: The gallows-maker; for that frame outlives a thousand tenants.

First Clown: I like thy wit well. . . . To't again, come.

Second Clown: Who builts stronger than a mason, a shipwright or a carpenter? I cannot tell.

First Clown: When you are asked this question next, say a grave-maker; the houses that he makes last till Doomsday.

Or the talk by the camp-fire before Agincourt when Henry V, not recognized by the men, argues with them.

Alexander Court: Brother, John Bates, is not that the morning which breaks younder?

Bates: I think it be: but we have no great cause to desire the approach of day.

Williams: We see yonder the beginning of the day, but I think we shall never see the end of it.

King Henry: I think the king is but a man as I am: the violet smells to him as it does to me . . . yet no man should possess him with any appearance of fear, lest he by showing it, should dishearten his army.

Bates: He may show what outward courage he will, but I believe, as cold a night as 'tis, he could wish himself in the Thames up to the neck—and so I wish he were, and I by him, so we were quit here.

King Henry: By my troth, I will speak my conscience of the king: I think he would not wish himself anywhere but where he is.

Bates: Then I would he were here alone; so should he be sure to be ransomed, and a many poor men's lives saved.

Williams: 'Tis certain, every man that dies ill, the ill upon his own head—the king is not to answer it.

Bates: I do not desire he should answer for me; and yet I determine to fight lustily for him.

King Henry: I myself heard the king say he would not be ransomed.

Williams: Ay, he said so, to make us fight cheerfully, but when our throats are cut he may be ransomed, and we ne'er the wiser.

King Henry: If I live to see it, I will never trust his word after.

Williams: You'll pay him them! That a perilous shot, out of an elder-gun, that's a poor and a private displeasure can do against a monarch! . . . You'll never trust his word after! Come, 'tis a foolish saying.

Leaving now the truly great in literature, let us take examples from the novelists. Turn to Jane Austen, and in *Emma* we find the following:

Mr. Woodhouse is discussing Emma's going to a dinner party: "We must remember to let James know the carriage will be wanted on Tuesday . . . and tell him what time you would have him come for you again; and you had better name an early hour. You will not like staying late."

"But you would not wish me to come away before I am tired, Papa?"

"Oh, no, my love, but you will soon be tired. There will be a great many people talking at once. You will not like the noise."

"But, my dear sir," cried Mr. Weston, "if Emma comes away early it will break up the party."

"And no great harm if it does," said Mr. Woodhouse, "the sooner every party breaks up, the better."

Or the never-to-be-forgotten talk between Mr. and Mrs. John Dashwood on the financial help to be given Mr. Dashwood's widowed stepmother and her three daughters.

"It was my father's last request to me that I should assist his widow and daughters."

"He did not know what he was talking of I dare say; ten to one but he was lightheaded at the time. Had he been in his right senses, he would not have thought of such a thing as begging you to give away half your fortune from your own child."

"The promise was given and must be performed. Something must be done for them whenever they leave Norland and settle in a new home."

"Well then, let something be done; but that something need not be three thousand pounds. Consider, when the money is once parted with, it never can return. If indeed it would ever be restored to our poor little boy."

"Why, to be sure, that would make a great difference . . . perhaps it would be better for all parties if the sum were diminished one half . . . as it is they will each have about three thousand pounds on their mother's death. . . ."

"That is very true, and I do not know whether upon the whole it would not be more advisable to do something for their mother while she lives, rather than for them—something of the annuity kind I mean. . . . I shall not bind myself to allow them anything yearly. To be tied down to the regular payment of such a sum is by no means desirable; it takes away one's independence. It may be very inconvenient some years."

"I believe you are right; it will be better that there should be no annuity in this case . . . a present of fifty pounds, now and then . . . will be amply discharging my promise to my father."

"To be sure it will. Indeed to say truth, I am convinced within myself that your father had no idea of you giving them any money at all."

"Upon my word, I believe you are perfectly right, and I will strictly fulfil my engagement by acts of kindness such as you have described. When my mother moves into another house my services shall be readily given to accommodate her as far as I can."

Here is one of Jane Austen's heroines who actually discusses the topic of how to talk to people on a first introduction. Elizabeth, in *Pride and Prejudice*, prepares to play the piano, and is talking to Colonel Fitzwilliam when Darcy comes up:

"You mean to frighten me, Mr. Darcy, by coming in all this state to hear me? But I will not be alarmed though your sister *does* play so well. There is a stubbornness about me that can never bear to be frightened at the will of others. My courage always rises with every attempt to intimidate me."

"I shall not say you are mistaken, because you would not really believe me to entertain any idea of alarming you, and I have had the pleasure of your acquaintance long enough to know that you find great enjoyment in occasionally professing opinions which are not in fact your own."

Elizabeth laughed heartily at this picture of herself, then (teasing Darcy as to his not having danced at the Netherfield ball)—

"He danced only four dances, though gentlemen were scarce. . . . Mr. Darcy, you cannot deny the fact."

"I had not at that time the honour of knowing any lady in the assembly beyond my own party."

"True, and nobody can ever be introduced in a ballroom."

"Perhaps," said Darcy, "I should have judged better, how I

sought an introduction, but I am ill qualified to recommend myself to strangers."

"Shall we ask your cousin the reason of this?" said Elizabeth, addressing Colonel Fitzwilliam. "Shall we ask him, why a man of sense and education, and who has lived in the world, is ill qualified to recommend himself to strangers?"

"I can answer your question," said Fitzwilliam, "without applying to him. It is because he will not give himself the trouble."

"I certainly have not the talent which some people possess," said Darcy, "of conversing easily with those I have never seen before. I cannot catch their tone of conversation, or appear interested in their concerns, as I often see done."

"My fingers," said Elizabeth, "do not move over this instrument in the masterly manner which I see so many people's do . . . but then I have always supposed it to be my fault—because I would not take the trouble of practising. It is not that I do not believe my fingers are as capable as any other woman's of superior execution." Darcy smiled and said: "You are perfectly right. You have employed your time much better. No one admitted to the privilege of hearing you, can think anything wanting. We neither of us perform to strangers."

Now a very different girl, Jane Eyre, in Charlotte Brontë's novel, also deals with "conversation."

Jane has been summoned by Rochester, who is bored.

"I have sent for you, the fire and the chandelier were not sufficient company for me, nor would Pilot [the dog] have been, for none of these can talk . . . it would please me now to draw you out—to learn more of you—therefore speak."

Instead of speaking I smiled, and not a very complacent or submissive smile either.

"Speak," he urged.

"What about, sir?"

"Whatever you like. I leave both the choice, and subject, and the manner of treating it entirely to yourself."

Accordingly I sat and said nothing. "If he expects me to talk for the mere sake of talking and showing off, he will find he has addressed himself to the wrong person," I thought.

"You are dumb, Miss Eyre."

I was dumb still. He bent his head a little towards me, and with a single hasty glance seemed to dive into my eyes.

"Stubborn?" he said, "and annoyed. Ah! it is consistent. I put my request in an absurd, almost insolent form . . . talk to me and divert my thoughts which are galled into dwelling on one point—cankering as a rusty nail. . . ."

"I am willing to amuse you if I can, sir: quite willing; but I cannot introduce a topic, because how do I know what will interest you; Ask me questions, and I will do my best to answer them."

In the Barchester novels of Anthony Trollope we have in Mrs. Proudie the supreme example of the style of a bullying, hectoring woman. Here she is, dealing with the flirtation of Signora Neroni and Mr. Slope.

"Mr. Slope, his lordship is especially desirous of your attendance below; you will greatly oblige me if you will join him. . . ." She stalked out.

"Is she always like this?" said the Signora.

"Yes—always—madam," said Mrs. Proudie returning, "always the same—always equally adverse to impropriety and conduct of every description," and she stalked back again.

"Mr. Slope," catching the delinquent at the door, "I am surprised you should leave my company to attend on such a painted Jezebel as that."

"But she's lame, Mrs. Proudie, and cannot move."

"Lame!" said Mrs. Proudie. "I'd lame her if she belonged to me. What business had she here at all?—such impertinence—such affectation."

Or here she is browbeating the poor bishop.

"I am told," said Mrs. Proudie, speaking very slowly, "that Mr. Slope is looking to be the new dean."

"Yes, certainly, I believe he is," said the bishop. "Mr. Slope spoke to me. It is very arrogant of him, I must say, but that is nothing to me."

"Arrogant!" said Mrs. Proudie. "It is the most impudent piece of pretension I ever heard of in my life. And what did you do in the matter, Bishop?"

"Why, my dear, I did speak to the Archbishop."

"You don't mean to tell me that you are going to make yourself ridiculous by lending your name to such a preposterous attempt as this?"

"It is preposterous, my dear."

"Then why have you endeavoured to assist him?"

"Why, my dear, I haven't assisted him much."

"But why have you done it at all? Why have you mixed your name up in anything so ridiculous? What was it you did say to the Archbishop?"

"I forget how I put it—would take it if he could get it—something of that sort. I didn't say more than that."

"You shouldn't have said anything at all. . . . Why did you think about it, Bishop? How could you think of making such a creature as that Dean of Barchester? Dean of Barchester indeed! I'll dean him!"

Suppose now we leave the novelists and turn instead to a very different sort of book. What can be more delightful than the absurd conversations of *Alice in Wonderland*?

Alice is greeted by the Caterpillar.

"Who are you?" said the Caterpillar. This was not an encouraging opening for a conversation. Alice replied rather shyly: "I—I hardly know at present. . . ."

"What do you mean by that?" said the Caterpillar sternly. "Explain yourself!"

"I can't explain myself, I'm afraid," said Alice, "because I'm not myself, you see."

"I don't see," said the Caterpillar.

". . . being so many different sizes in a day," said Alice, "is very confusing."

"It isn't," said the Caterpillar.

"Well, perhaps you haven't found it so yet," said Alice, "but when you have to turn into a chrysalis, and then after that into a butterfly, I should think you'll feel it a little queer, won't you?"

"Not a bit," said the Caterpillar.

"Well, perhaps your feelings may be different," said Alice, "but it would feel very queer to *me*."

"You!" said the Caterpillar contemptuously. "Who are you?"

Alice drew herself up: "I think you ought to tell me who *you* are, first."

"Why?" said the Caterpillar.

As Alice could not think of any good reason, and as the Caterpillar seemed to be in a *very* unpleasant state of mind, she turned away.

"Come back!" the Caterpillar called after her. "I've something important to say!"

Alice turned and came back again.

"Keep your temper," said the Caterpillar.

Or Alice and Humpty Dumpty.

"We may start fresh," said Humpty Dumpty. "And it's my turn to choose a subject. ("He talks about it just as if it were a game!" thought Alice.) "So here's a question for you. How old did you say you were?"

Alice made a short calculation, and said: "Seven years and six months."

"Wrong!" Humpty Dumpty exclaimed triumphantly. "You never said a word like it!"

"I thought you meant: 'How old *are* you?'" Alice explained.

"If I'd meant that I'd have said it," said Humpty Dumpty.

Alice didn't want to begin another argument, so she said nothing.

"An uncomfortable sort of age!" said Humpty Dumpty. "Now, if you'd asked my advice, I'd have said: 'Leave off at seven'— but it's too late now."

"I never ask advice about growing," Alice said indignantly.

"Too proud?" the other inquired.

"I meant," said Alice, "one can't help growing older."

"*One* can't perhaps," said Humpty Dumpty, "but *two* can. With proper assistance you might have left off at seven."

These conversations which accompany Alice's journeys through "Wonderland" are pure fantasy, but there is rather the same element of mad reality in those dialogues which are meant to be useful to travellers in the real world. We all know the helpful little books which give us "model" conversations to help us in trying to talk to foreigners abroad.

Here are some passages from *The Traveller's Pocket Companion,* written a hundred and fifty years ago by Madame de Genlis, as dialogues, or conversations, on various occasions.

On Paying a Visit. (Somebody knocks.) "Go and see who it is!" "It is Mrs. B." "Good morning! I am very glad to see you." "How are you?" "Pretty well, I thank you." "I have not seen you this age." "You are quite a stranger." "Do sit down." "And how does your mother?" "She is not very well." "I am sorry for it." "And how does your brother?" "I believe he is well." "I rejoice to hear that." "Where is he?" "In the country." "And where is your sister?" "She is gone out." "Will you stay and take dinner with us?" "I cannot stay." "Why are you in such a hurry?" "I have a great many things to do." "Surely you can stay a little longer?" "I will stay longer another time."

On Board a Ship. "I think we shall have a storm, what is your opinion?" "I feel very sick." "Lay yourself flat upon your face, shut your eyes, remain in that quiet posture, and your sickness will abate." "I suffer extremely, please reach me the basin." "I advise you to take a few Hoffmark's drops. Here is the vial of the drops." "My head pains me very much; I have a shivering all over me." "That is the effects of the sea-sickness, you must not be uneasy on that account." "The wind gets higher. Do you think there is any danger?" "I have tooth-ache!" "That happens frequently at sea."

Conversation at an Inn. "Do you wish for a room with two beds?" "Yes, I should like one on the first floor. I dislike the ground floor because it is damp and dark.

Give me a snug quiet apartment. Does anybody move above me? I dislike most of all noise over my head. There is a disagreeable smell in this room. It must be swept out and scented with vinegar. . . . This coverlet is dirty. It is too heavy. Bring some good clean sheets. I must tell you I shall examine them very carefully. These sheets have clearly been used already. They are damp. I will not have them. I must have some others. I have my own sheets but I always have sheets from the Inn in order to spread them over the mattress, afterwards I spread my own over them."

A completely modern book, Lyall's *Languages of Europe,* gives the same picture.

" 'Good evening, have you a cheap single room?' 'No, sir, only a double room.' 'Where is the key of my room?' 'Upstairs in the door.' 'Please prepare me a hot bath, and bring me some soap.' 'There is no towel . . . bring me a small flask of brandy and some fresh tea.' 'These eggs are bad.' 'What is the name of this place?' 'It is very beautiful, isn't it?' 'Please send for the best doctor here. I have a headache. I think I am ill . . . how much is this?' 'It is too much.' 'I am sorry.' 'Goodbye.' "

Well, we can all see these limited, stilted remarks are just the sort of "conversation" which should not be made, but can we anywhere find models which show us what conversation can be? Modern plays, which consist entirely of dialogue, should possibly give us some idea, but the best are beyond us, they are too sparkling for us ever to hope we can imitate them, though we may enviously admire their brilliance.

Oscar Wilde's *Importance of Being Earnest* gives us the style of conversation of the late nineteenth century, G. B. Shaw is the model for the beginning of the twentieth, and just as Noël Coward represents the period between the wars, T. S. Eliot's *Cock-tail Party*, though written in verse, shows us the dialogue of the present day. If we get these plays and read them we can appreciate the extreme brilliance and subtlety of conversation which flashes from one speaker to another. This is "conversation as a fine art," which shows us what heights it can reach— but they are probably too far beyond our reach.

We can learn nothing from films, which indeed provide no real conversations. Such talk as there is bears on the action. Perhaps this is a pointer for us, since in reading plays we come to appreciate words and how to use them. In the films we lose our sense of their importance.

The radio, again, gives us no "good conversation" except in the very rare instances of "Imaginary Conversations" between great figures of the past. "Mrs. Dale's Diary," popular as it is, and "The Archers," are features which consist of dialogue, of talks going on between different people, but they deal solely with little day-to-day events. It is noticeable the characters are dealing only with their personal problems, they never talk of anything else. No, if we want models of good conversation we must go to the best writers.

CHAPTER SIXTEEN

SUMMARY

Summary — don'ts and do's — do not lay down the law — show off — snub — lose your temper — be silent — monopolize conversation — talk about yourself. — Do's — be polite — reasonable — calm — take your share — be sincere — develop ideas — see other point of view — help others to enjoy themselves — practice makes perfect.

PERHAPS now some ways in which we can learn the art of conversation have become clear. For, firstly, there is one thing to bear in mind, conversation is an art and can be learnt. People who honestly wish they could become "good talkers" have to realize they must make efforts. The naturally gifted and highly intelligent people have their way made easier, though, as we have seen, more than "brains" is needed. For those who do not have such natural gifts it is clear they must be prepared to make efforts.

If you are to talk well and interestingly you must of course have plenty to talk about, real subjects. Obviously people with wide interests will have more to talk about, and for them the finding of a subject will not be hard. People who find it difficult and say: "I never can think of anything to talk about," have to grasp the fact that they must be ready to take pains over this. Indeed, it often seems as though the first and supreme difficulty people feel is: "What can I talk about?" They just think despairingly that they have nothing interesting they *can* talk about. Granted that it is a difficulty, it is one which has to be faced and overcome. Different people will tackle it in different ways. Often you hear people say:

"But I've such a dull life," or: "I'm such a dull person," "I can't interest other people." That is being too modest, or too despairing. What seems dull to you may not be at all dull to other people. So often things that crop up in the course of a day's work are not interesting to you, you take them as a matter of course, but they may be interesting to other people whose lives are quite different. For instance, a lift-man, or a bus conductor, or anyone working in a shop, may think of everything that happens to them as quite dull. Yet they see a great deal of other people, they know how people behave, they notice odd people or odd events, and people who live at home, or have routine jobs, would envy them their chances of talking about what goes on and how people behave. Housewives, who think of themselves as "shut up between the walls of their house," would envy those who go about. Yet housewives, too, can find they have their own variety of happenings. The trips to the shops can produce something to talk of, the things that happen in the road, the changes in the countryside, the flowers in other people's gardens; there are really plenty of little chances here to find subjects.

It may not come easily to "bring them in," but at least everyone can be ready to try to think of something he could say, and venture on it in the hope the others may find it something they like to hear about.

If all that seems too trivial, then those who desperately want to set themselves up with subjects for conversation must go about it quite seriously. They must, disagreeable as it may sound, try quite definitely to "improve" themselves. For example, a good many people glance at a newspaper to see the news items, but every paper today has a leading article which gives the expression of opinion on the topics of today. It is easy to get ideas from them, either one agrees or disagrees, but it is an opinion and therefore can be argued about. Or—worse still this may seem—one can make an effort to learn about subjects one has never thought of. In any of our cities today there are museums and galleries, and many people go to them. If you try this you will at least be trying something new—and if you hate it and are bored, well, you can talk about how you disliked it and what a waste of time it was! Of course, if you find you enjoy it, the best way to help yourself still further is to get some book on what you have seen and try to understand more about it all. A great deal of enjoyment is missed because people think first: "Oh, that's so dull!" or even if they find it not altogether dull they do not try to go on and grow to enjoy such things by seeing more of them, comparing one place with another, and reading the books or pamphlets which are written nowadays and are on sale in these galleries.

One simple instance may illustrate this. The driver of a hired car was often employed to drive people round to see various interesting churches in a country neighbourhood. He never went into any of them, he sat outside, until one day one of the passengers suggested he came along, too. He was first rather bored, then as they went from one to another, rather interested, until in the end he became an enthusiast and really began to read and study the architecture and history of such buildings. This may be an idea which will not appeal to many; but there is the fact to be faced, you cannot possibly hope to be interesting to other people, or to talk interestingly, if you just make no effort at all to be interested in anything outside yourself.

Again, it has to be remembered that none of these "improvements" come all of a sudden. You have to go on trying and searching for interests. This is one of the first things in which people can, by taking pains, improve. If you are fond of reading, then try to remember, as you read, that a book or something in a book has interested you, and you can keep that in your mind as something you would like to talk about. If you are not fond of reading, then you must bestir yourself and think over things which do interest you, and be prepared to talk about them. You may have to try out in your mind how you think this can be done. To take a simple example if you are fond of animals or birds, do not just imagine yourself saying: "I've a grand dog," or "a budgerigar that talks." You need to remember half your battle is to give the person to whom you talk something to say in return. So you can think, perhaps, that you will go on to discuss the merits of dogs as against those of cats, or the breed you prefer, or going to a dog- or cat-show and the advantages of keeping dogs in towns, and the rules against having them in flats and so on.

Or if you have no such special tastes, you can think of talking about holidays—what makes a good holiday, is it better to go to a quiet place or a gay seaside resort? Is it possible to make a trip abroad? Should families go together? And so on. It is a help to try to think along these lines beforehand, taking any subject you fancy and trying to see what you can make of it, always being sure you are, however simply or even vaguely, looking for ways in which you can go along talking about your subject and getting it a bit further.

Probably you ought to think out two or three topics in this way. For naturally no one wants to go on talking about one thing only. You use up the subject, it becomes dull, and you come to a full stop. Here, of course, the two people (or more) talking together ought to help each other. It should not be left all on one side. If you are not actually the person to begin the conversation, you have an equally important part to play, for you must respond, you must try to follow up, too, add your ideas, make your contribution. It is very hard work if one talks and the other just barely replies: "Oh! how nice," or "How interesting," or "I haven't thought about it." Conversation is like a duet, both must share and play their part. Even if one person can talk easily he still will not want to be talking to anyone who really makes no effort and adds nothing to the conversation. So if each tries to realize that he simply must help, then of course it becomes easier. No one ought to feel that he by himself has to make all the conversation, everyone should be able to reckon that other people will take a share. Just as when you play cards you reckon you can count on some support from your partner, so you should feel you will get some sort of support in your efforts to talk. Whenever you hear people say: "I do enjoy a talk with So-and-so, he is so interesting, he has lots to talk about," you can say to yourself: "Well, I must find lots to talk about." Because these people who are interesting have not just been born with plenty of things to discuss, they have actually spent their time in acquiring knowledge. They have either read, or gone about, or had hobbies and interests—sewing, bee-keeping, photography, gardening, all sorts and kinds of things have they taken up. They have, so to speak, a store of subjects on which to draw. Well, everyone can try to collect such a store. If your mind is empty, of course you will not talk well, so you have to try to collect or develop your ideas. You can develop interests, and that stores your mind, and you then have the true foundation of conversation.

That leads us to some of the things you ought to make up your mind you must *not* do if you want to carry on conversations. You must not be silent, you must not be content to listen and avoid saying much. No one wants to be labelled as "dull—never opens his mouth." You must resolve you will always try to respond, to "play-up" to whatever is being talked about, and try to add something to the subject. It is useless to excuse yourself by saying you are "shy" or "nervous" or "too stupid." As we have seen, these *are* excuses; everyone can produce something to say if he will only be brave and make an effort. People always forgive the shy, and however you stumble and stutter they will listen and try to help you, and all those obstacles can be overcome if you just stick doggedly to your resolution and do your best. You will improve in time, it is the first efforts that are the worst. Indeed, almost all people are shy to start with, but those who make steady efforts to get over their shyness do succeed. Sometimes, too, people who have done this appear on the surface as perfectly easy and bright, and only when you get to know them well will they surprise you by saying they started life as terribly shy, and still may feel so, only they have learnt not to show it. Quite often, when you get to know people, they will tell you how they still are nervous if they meet new people, or go to a new place, and you may say: "Well, I never would have guessed that." It simply means they have trained themselves to get over this common difficulty, and have done it so well people do not realize anything. Nerve yourself to imitate that example.

It is also true that if you tend to be silent and not join in a conversation, that is a habit which will grow on you. You'll become accustomed to sit and listen, and it will get harder and harder for you to break that habit. You will end by being known as someone who "never utters"—and that will mean people are blaming you. They will feel you ought to take your share, and so you should. You are really lazy and selfish, though you may not realize that.

The cleverest people are actually quite often disappointing as talkers. If one is fortunate enough to be asked to meet well-known persons—writers, politicians, soldiers and so on—frequently one is disappointed, they have seemed ordinary, even dull. This may be because though they are brilliant where their work is concerned, and have won their great reputations because of it, yet they may take little or no interest in anything outside it. Or they may be thoroughly tired of being expected to shine in company; they do not want to be exhibited as famous, nor do they wish it to be taken for granted they will sparkle or impress when they meet other people. Even more simply, they may be shy and reserved, they may be quite incapable of making small talk, or entering into casual conversation, and this may be made worse for them by the very fact that they know quite well people are hoping a great deal from meeting them. So let this console the "ordinary" man or woman. You are not the mental equal of the very distinguished, but it is within the bounds of possibility that you may be able to enter into conversation more happily—and in a more carefree way—than they do! A really clever woman who had simple, natural ways once said how often people she met would say to her innocently afterwards: "Well, I

never would have thought you were a clever woman."
What they meant, of course, was they had not been
nervous or overawed. She said she never quite knew
whether she was vexed at the idea that "clever" people
were terrifying and therefore disagreeable, or pleased
that she had not proved to be either, but that in any
case she was always glad she had been treated as a
perfectly ordinary person. For exceptional people may
have just that feeling, they are a little cut off from
"ordinary" people, there is a sort of barrier between
them and the rest of the world. So they are only too
thankful and pleased to be treated as no different from
anyone else, and to be expected to talk on the perfectly
ordinary simple subjects that interest most men and
women.

However, if silence, shyness and unwillingness to take
part in a conversation are bad, the opposite is true, too;
people must not talk so much that no one else gets a
chance. This is not as usual a thing as shyness, but we do
all know people who "don't let you get a word in edge-
ways," or of whom it is said: "She's a terrible talker; it
wears me out to listen to her." This is a fault which,
where it exists, grows worse as time goes on. People get
to "love to hear the sound of their own voices," and they
are so pleased to hear them they get more and more into
the habit of talking on and on. They may become so used
to it that it is difficult for them to check themselves.
Quite often people do vaguely realize it, and will say
apologetically: "I'm afraid I'm a great talker." Well, if
they realize that at all, they can take steps to check
themselves. Indeed, the most determined talker can see,
if he just uses his eyes, that he ought to check this flow.
The persons to whom he is talking will certainly, sooner

or later, show in their faces that they are getting tired
and bored. Their eyes begin to wander round the room,
they begin to try to listen with half an ear to other
conversations. The signs are really there, if only the great
talker will notice them and realize that his stream of
words is not any longer being attended to. Again, it is a
matter of practice and of training. Never go on too long.
Always let someone else have a chance. Be sure you do
not monopolize the conversation.

This ought to be specially heeded by those who are
naturally amusing and clever, and also by those who have
interesting lives and have all sorts of interesting experiences. One very clever woman gradually became someone to be dreaded at any party or wherever anyone met
her. For she simply "took the floor," talked away without
ceasing, on what she was doing, who she had met, what
a splendid day she had had, and so on. At first this
was quite entertaining, for she had many amusing and
interesting things to tell, but she let the habit grow on
her, until she literally would let no one else talk, and
her voice, always talking about herself, would flow on
and on without stopping. She spoilt everyone's pleasure
and in the end became a bore and a nuisance.

That was the case of someone who was actually clever
and nice, and whose conversation would have been
delightful if she had checked herself, but a less agreeable
and more dangerous habit is that of "laying down the
law." Chattering on and on is just tiring to others, but
to talk to anyone who lays down the law makes the
listeners cross and leads to trouble. For no one likes to
be treated as ignorant or stupid. They do not want to
be told: "Now, I know all about this, let me just tell
you that . . ." or: "You can take it from me that . . ."

Bald statements: "He's a fool, knows nothing about it,"
followed by an account of how the speaker himself
knows *all* about it, and that *his* views and opinions cannot
be questioned, make the listener often rebel. He knows
in advance it will not be any good arguing, for the very
self-assertive person will not wish to have his views and
theories questioned and will be offended. Too often those
confident people are not opposed, and they get more
and more into the habit of "talking down" others and
always taking it for granted that what they say is right
and cannot be disputed. So if you find the slightest
tendency of this sort in yourself, check it. Learn to say:
"But that is only what I think, and you may not agree?"
or: "That's my opinion, as far as it goes, but perhaps
I'm wrong?" Never think that you must be right and
that anyone who does not agree with you is stupid.

Here, as always, any sort of conceit or showing-off
always aggravates and annoys others. So one of the
"don'ts" in conversation must be don't praise yourself,
don't describe how you've distinguished yourself. Don't
think—for that is a form of conceit, too—that others will
always be interested to hear what you've been doing, or
how cleverly you managed something. You may quite
often hear someone say: "But I was too cute, I knew how
to get the better of that," or: "I was clever enough to
see through that, so I tell you what I did," and so on.
That is only indirect boasting. Naturally every now and
then there is something you've done or said which will
quite rightly amuse others to hear. But, as in the other
cases, that way of talking grows on people, they tend
more and more to talk of their clever ways in getting
what they want, and if they do this too much they
become bores and no one wants to listen to them.

Those faults which spoil conversation are in the nature of habits, people are, to begin with, unconscious of them, and it is only because they tend to grow and increase that they become in time so bad. But there is another group of "don'ts" which are not exactly habits, but which come from real faults in disposition. Such as snubbing other people and losing one's temper. Men or women may have a sarcastic way of speaking, they are contemptuous of what other people say. If they hear anyone say anything rather stupid or silly they pounce down at once and crush the unhappy offender. They may not be downright rude, but they do really intend to "set down" the other person, and perhaps think to themselves how clever their crushing remark has been. Well, that is really a horrid characteristic. People who are inclined to be sarcastic had better try to curb themselves if they want to be good at conversation. Children and young people always loathe sarcasm, they cannot bear to be made to feel "a fool"—neither can grown-ups. They may be forced to bear with it, and they may not feel themselves able to stand up to it, or reply. But they will resent it, and the clever person who snubs or makes others feel ridiculous will come to be dreaded. It is a temptation to use a clever, sharp tongue, but it is one that must be resisted with might and main. To lose one's temper is equally bad, and equally clearly spoils any talk, but it does at least bring its own punishment at once. People who grow angry, and lose their tempers, do afterwards have the dreadful knowledge that they ought not to have done so. They are ashamed of having made an exhibition of themselves, they are probably ashamed of the things they said, and of their loss of control. Some people know they cannot argue without losing their tempers. Well, if that is so, then they must make a rule not to get drawn into an argument, or perhaps not to let themselves argue on certain things which they know make them angry. Avoid such subjects. Say, if they come up: "Well, we'd better not talk about that, because it makes me angry and I can't argue about it without losing my temper." It is a little sad if we cannot really learn to control ourselves; but if we honestly cannot, then let us recognize it and not join in a conversation which we know too well will end in trouble.

That brings us to the things we ought to try to do. First, and most naturally, to be polite. To be ready to listen, to be willing to disagree politely, and always to be sure we are not going to offend or hurt people's feelings. In fact, consider other people's feelings all along the line. If you really train yourself always to be polite, reasonable, and so to speak gentle, in arguments or talks, you ensure the conversation will be amiable. If you can, do keep calm even if you violently disagree with what is being said. Do not get excited, remember that vehemence or strong speaking will not appeal to others. Everyone can enjoy arguing with a reasonable person who talks calmly, and if everyone is certain that you will argue peacefully and reasonably they will enjoy it. It is a great pleasure to hear, for instance, on the radio, people having an argument with perfect good temper, each letting the other state his case, and answering in a reasonable way. Just as we occasionally experience in listening to those debates how hopeless it is when one or other, or both, gets angry, loses his temper, and usually ends by simply being rude!

Consideration for others, shown by being careful in the actual way we speak, needs to go further, as we have seen earlier. You must think of the other people in trying to carry on a conversation, you must take your share, you must help things along, you must be extra willing to encourage anyone who is shy and awkward. You must not just be thinking of yourself, you must be thinking of the other persons. Start off by wondering how you can interest them, what is likely to interest and amuse them as a subject. Begin by trying to discover what they do, what they like, and talk about that. If you find you have struck someone who will not respond, who is too shy or who is "difficult to talk to," because he has few interests, then you must launch out on your own and start off on something that interests you, and see if that will interest him as well.

To take the simplest kind of example. People sometimes complain that the English always talk about the weather; well, it is true we often do begin on it, but partly because it is "safe" as an opening, and you go on from there. You may say: "Hasn't it been a lovely day?" or: "Wasn't yesterday awful, raining all the time" —but you can go on from there to find out what the other person was doing that day, what he prefers in the way of weather—heat, cold, wind or what, how does he amuse himself on a wet holiday?—and you have made a beginning toward discovering his tastes, his amusements and his interests.

Again, we saw how one must be sincere, must be frank, have courage enough to say what we really think and feel. If you really like to "laze about and do nothing" on a wet day, well say so, and explain why you find that more of a rest than occupying yourself. If you always enjoy going to the cinema, even to a poor film, say so, and why you can enjoy practically any film.

If you do not enjoy reading, say so, only never pretend, be frank and say what you think and feel.

Try to get into the way of seeing what is interesting in other people's ideas. Try to exchange knowledge, talk of what you know and do your best to follow up what other people say. Let them see you want to be interested in them and their thoughts. If they want to talk about something in which you are not very interested—if, for example, you are not at all interested in gardening or sport—at least let them talk about their subject and see if you cannot find something in what they say that is interesting. Then, when you think they have had a good spell on their pet subject, you can try to get them to be interested in yours. As long as you are trying hard to please and amuse them you will probably discover you are interested in spite of yourself. You may find, too, that even if at first the subject itself does not interest you, it may lead on to better ground if you persevere. You can progress from gardens, or sport, to the pleasure of "outdoor" things. You can work round from a football match to discussing the watching of sport, or of the sports you yourself enjoy. It all depends on how you try to answer and talk about a subject which to begin with you thought dull.

Indeed, here we come to what is really the truth about the art of conversation. It depends very largely on plain unselfishness. Thinking of other people's pleasure, thinking of any obvious disadvantage they may have such as shyness, helping them to talk, trying to get over your own faults. Thinking whether you are lazy in doing your share, or if you are not trying hard enough to get over your own awkwardness. Thinking how you can gain new knowledge, get hold of new ideas, not missing chances in your daily life of storing up something—however small—which might be interesting to others, or that might make you a better-informed, a more alert and so a more "interesting person." This may sound rather a toilsome thing, or it may sound rather "priggish" and "improving." It is not really, for no one wants to be dull, and no one need be, but he will be if he does not try to gain as much, try to get the best out of himself, as he possibly can. Then, if you really have made efforts to know about things, to read, to use your eyes and notice things, to be interested in other people, and all that goes on in daily life, and in the outside world, you do really become a more interesting person yourself. As a result you will perhaps one day have people say: "You do talk of interesting things," or: "I like talking to you, you are so interested in everything," or: "You're always interested in other people."

It may be that seems a difficult way to have to go to work, and one may feel that however much one tries one will not succeed very well; but the most encouraging thing about the art of conversation is that if you try, if you keep on and persevere, you do make progress. Practice does make perfect. You may get along slowly. You may find it hard to get started. You may almost despair and think: "I never shall learn, I shall never have enough to talk about."

That, however, is all wrong. The one certain thing is that if you try you will in the end succeed. Some are born "brilliant," but they are the few. Everyone who wishes to be able to carry on conversation can try, and he can set himself the task of trying to be a person who wants, not to impress other people, but just to give them pleasure. If you think of others, and not of yourself, if you do not worry as to whether they will think you clever, or stupid, if you try not to think of yourself at all, but just how you can make the other person enjoy himself, you will make a good conversationalist.